Rose and Lotus

TONGLIN LU

ROSE

AND

LOTUS

Narrative of Desire in France and China

STATE UNIVERSITY OF NEW YORK PRESS

Published by
State University of New York Press, Albany

For information, address State University of New York
Press, State University Plaza, Albany, N.Y., 12246

Library of Congress Cataloging-in-Publication Data
Lu, Tonglin.
    Rose and lotus : narrative of desire in France and China / Tonglin
  Lu.
        p.   cm.
    Includes bibliographical references.
    ISBN 0–7914–0463–3 (alk. paper). — ISBN 0–7914–0464–1 (pbk. :
  alk. paper)
    1. French fiction—18th century—History and criticism.
2. Literature, Comparative—French and Chinese.   3. Literature,
Comparative—Chinese and French.   4. Chinese fiction—History and
criticism.   5. Desire in literature.   6. Sex in literature.
I. Title.
PQ637.D38L8   1990
843′.5093538—dc20   90–9599
                                                               CIP

10 9 8 7 6 5 4 3 2 1

*To my father, Lu Zheng-cao, and my mother, Liu Sha.
Perhaps they deserve a more "decent" subject or a better book.
But as a Chinese old saying tells us: "A mother does not dislike her
child's ugliness." Moreover, this book on desire is dedicated with love.*

Contents

To what extent does the East differ from the West? May we grasp some of their differences through a comparison of their forms of eroticism, exemplified by their flower-symbols: the rose and the lotus? These are questions to which I would like to find answers through this book.

This book studies two aspects of sexuality in narrative: the positive (idealized or sublimated) and the negative (destructive or perverse) aspects. I have chosen as the object of my analysis two eighteenth-century French novels, *Julie, ou la Nouvelle Héloïse* and *Les Liaisons dangereuses,* and two classic Chinese novels, *The Golden Lotus* and *The Dream of the Red Chamber.*

As all four books were written before cultural exchanges between China and the West became frequent, the French and the Chinese works are free of mutual influences. Moreover, each of the four novels can be taken as representative of the portrayal of one aspect of sexuality in fiction of a given historical and cultural context, thanks to their success as literary works and to the influence on their readership.

Les Liaisons dangereuses and *The Golden Lotus* can be paired together, since both describe the destructive side of sexual desire. *Julie, ou la Nouvelle Héloïse* and *The Dream of the Red Chamber* are likewise similar in their exaltation of spiritual love. However, these apparent analogies only make the fundamental differences between the Eastern and Western novels more striking. In fact, my analysis emphasizes the dissimilarities of the paired novels more than their similarities.

Why is eroticism in French novels generally conceptualized as it is in Choderlos de Laclos's libertine novel, whereas eroticism in Chinese premodern fiction tends to be much less self-conscience as in Lan-ling Hsiao-hsiao sheng's *The Golden Lotus*? Why does the rhetoric of love play a much more important role in Jean-Jacques Rousseau's *Julie, ou la Nouvelle Héloïse* than in Ts'ao Hsüeh-ch'in's *The Dream of the Red Chamber*?

In order to answer these questions, I try to analyze the role played by sexuality in the relationship between self and society in these four novels.

According to Georges Bataille, eroticism is a form of transgression against the norms that determine individual behavior in a given society. At the same time, eroticism itself is largely determined by its object of transgression: social norms. Idealized love may be considered to be a sublimated form of eroticism. In many respects, spiritual love represents an aesthetic vision of individualism in that it asserts the superiority of the beloved (or the mirror-image of the self) to his or her society.

To a large extent, these two forms of violation reflect the dominant ideological forces inherent in a given culture—either religion, as in the case of Christianity, reinterpreted through different intellectual and artistic movements, such as Neoclassicism, the Enlightenment and Preromanticism; or ethics, as in the case of Confucianism, transformed through Taoist and Buddhist influences. In the West, religion had to be secularized, and in the East, ethics mystified, in order for each to become a counterexample or a reverse mirror image of itself in the form of individualism.

Acknowledgments

I would like to express my gratitude to my professors at Princeton University. I am particularly indebted to Professor Lionel Gossman for his kindness, understanding, and generosity, without which this book would not have been materialized. I shall always remember Professor Kao Yu-kung's and Professor Andrew Plaks's insightful advice. Professor Earl Miner's gentle "paternalism" also made my study at Princeton enjoyable.

While my professors at Princeton have introduced me to the English-speaking academic world, my professors at the Université de Montréal initiated me into the realm of Western theory when I first came to North America. I owe special thanks to two of them, Timothy Reiss and Eugene Vance, for their valuable criticisms.

My discussions with Mihai Spariosu, my colleague at the University of Georgia, Rey Chow, my colleague at the University of Minnesota, and Maureen Robertson, my colleague at the University of Iowa, helped me to clarify certain conceptual obscurities. I am grateful to Ilene Cohen for her editing.

Among my friends at Princeton, I would like to thank Chuck Nunley, David Posner, Steven Wlodek, and Eric MacPhail for their proofreading. In addition, I would also like to express my gratitude for Jody Beenk for her assistance in the final stage of preparation of the manuscript. I am also grateful to Patty Cheng at the University of Minnesota and Alan Hellawell at Princeton University for helping me search for library references.

Note on Convention

Transliterated Chinese within the text is noted with a superscript alphabetical reference. The superscript letter (ie: *ch'ing*) refers the reader to the list of Chinese characters in the Appendix of Chinese Characters at the end of the book. Transliterations reappearing in the text are cross referenced to the first instance. These later citations are indicated in parentheses (ie: *ch'ing* (Int. b)) immediately following the transliterated term. For example, in the introduction, *ch'ing* tells the reader to see note b in the Glossary of Chinese Characters. In chapter 4, *ch'ing* (Int. b.) means the reader should go back to note b in the Appendix.

Introduction

The number of books dealing with the problem of sexuality
in Western literature is large, but it is difficult to find works on
the same subject in Chinese literature; to my knowledge, no
scholarly book has been written from a Chinese-French comparative perspective.

Sexual relations, however, must be a meaningful subject for
comparative study. Since on the one hand, sexual relations are
the most private matter in human life, yet, on the other hand,
one of the forms of human behavior most determined by culture,
sexuality offers a complex picture of the relationship between self
and society.

As Georges Bataille states in his *Erotism*, the difference between human and animal sexuality is that the former is limited
by prohibitions. According to the same author, the existence of
taboo is the source of the intense pleasure that human beings
may derive from sexual activities: "Desire in eroticism is the desire that triumphs over the taboo."[1] Since the taboo that shapes
the sexual behavior of an individual is formulated largely on the
basis of his or her cultural and social background, a study of sexuality may lead toward a consideration of certain characteristics
of a given culture.

Fiction is no doubt a privileged field in this respect. On the
one hand, sexuality has always been one of its favorite subjects in
France as well as in China. On the other hand, desire itself is
largely fictional.[2] In order to examine sexuality as portrayed in

the French and the Chinese novel, I have chosen as test cases two eighteenth-century French novels, *Julie, ou La Nouvelle Héloïse*[3] and *Les Liaisons dangereuses*,[4] and two traditional Chinese novels, *The Golden Lotus*[5] (*Chin P'ing Mei*)[a] and *The Dream of the Red Chamber*[6] (*Hung-lou meng*).[b]

Les Liaisons dangereuses and *The Golden Lotus* share a significant common characteristic: the negative or destructive attitude of their characters toward sexual relations. At the same time, *Julie, ou la Nouvelle Héloïse* and *The Dream of the Red Chamber* are both characterized by the sublimation of sexual desire in the form of idealized love.

At first glance, there may appear to be an anachronism in my choices. The two French novels and *The Dream of the Red Chamber* belong to the eighteenth century, whereas *The Golden Lotus* was written two centuries earlier.

The term "novel" in eighteenth-century France, however, does not mean exactly the same thing as the Chinese term *hsiao-shuo*[c] translated as "novel."

In the first place, the Chinese novel has different formal conventions. One of the terms that describes this form is the "chapter-divided novel" (*chang-hui hsiao-shuo*),[d] which has a pejorative connotation. It indicates a narrative form divided into a great number of chapters and implies that this form may not necessarily be conducive to a coherent structure. This term, as used by writers during the May Fourth Movement, favors the form of Western novels. But in reality, it is not fair to judge the Chinese novel in accordance with criteria derived from another narrative genre determined by different cultural, ideological, aesthetic, and ethical values.

Second, the evolution of the novel in China and in France, respectively, followed different courses. Whereas the French novel began to flourish in the eighteenth century and reached its apogee in the following century, the Chinese novel, which began to prosper two centuries earlier, has never occupied a position as overwhelmingly important as the French novel in its culture.

Although the Ming-Ch'ing period (fourteenth to nineteenth centuries) is considered the peak of the traditional Chinese novel, only six works are unanimously accepted by scholars as "classics." They are *The Three Kingdoms* (*san-kuo yan-yi*),[e] *Pilgrimage to the West (hsi-yu chi)*,[f] *Water Margin (Shui hu)*,[g] *The Golden Lotus (Chin P'ing Mei), The Scholars (Ju-lin wai-shih)*[h], and *The Dream of the Red Chamber (Hung-lou meng)*.[7] Naturally, these six novels are not necessarily the "best," as most scholarly works on the traditional Chinese novel have claimed, since the distinction between a "good" and a "bad" literary work has always been ideologically oriented. But for these works, the scholarly judgment is also based on their lasting popularity.

The plots in all these Chinese novels have been retold and readopted again and again in different forms of popular art, including storytelling, traditional opera and drama, film, and soap opera. Because of their relatively strong influence on a larger audience, which includes both intellectuals and street people, they may be considered more pregnant with certain cultural values. Among these six novels, *The Golden Lotus* and *The Dream of the Red Chamber* are the only two *romans de moeurs*. Both of them deal with the family life of ordinary people within the framework of a large household. Perhaps for the same reason, sexual relations occupy a central position in the two novels.

In spite of their differences, both the Chinese chapter-divided novel and the French novel are among the most important and complex narrative forms in their respective cultures. Historically speaking, there is also a common ground between sixteenth-century China and eighteenth-century France. Drawing sustenance from Renaissance thinkers such as Erasmus and from neoclassic thinkers such as Descartes, the French philosophers of the Enlightenment questioned and reinterpreted Christianity in the name of individual reason and the cult of knowledge. The rationalization of faith, led to a naturalization of supernaturalism, if not the secularization of religion, as Meyer H. Abrams describes.[8]

Conversely, in the sixteenth century, Wang Yang-ming, one of the masters of the School of the Mind, and his disciples also achieved a significant change in the reinterpretation of Confucianism. Chu Hsi,[9] in his theory "investigation of things" *(ke-wu)*[i] interpreted the Confucian Tao or principle in terms of rules existing in things or the objective world.

These rules, written in Confucian classics, were supposed to govern the moral behavior of each individual. Challenging the orthodox interpretation of Confucianism of his time, Wang Yang-ming claimed that principles exist in the mind in his concept of "achieving the innate knowledge" (*chih liang-chih*).[j]

In other words, the self was the center of the social and the natural worlds. One no longer needed to take recourse to external rules; the self-expression of a sincere mind had the highest moral value in Wang's interpretation of Confucianism. Confucian ethics were, for him, the manifestations of "innate goodness." In other words, Wang Yang-ming's interpretation of Confucianism is much more individualistic than his predecessor's, even though he tried to justify his individualism by ethicizing the human mind.

Furthermore, Wang Yang-ming's reinterpretation of Confucianism was influenced by his early Buddhist and Taoist studies, which contributed to a mystical tendency in his late interpretation of Confucian thought. The individualistic and pluralist reinterpretation of Christian faith in France led to a demystification of religion, whereas the same process in China had a tendency to mystification vis-à-vis Confucian ethics. In each case, the intellectual reform in regard to the dominant ideology was accompanied by the prosperity of narrative.

Even though Hans-Georg Gadamer may be overstating the case when he says that the transgression of a tradition is, more than anything else, determined by the tradition itself,[10] the relationship between the object of subversion and the subversive force is much more complicated than a mere opposition.

On the one hand, in spite of the polemical attitude of certain philosophers, such as Denis Diderot and Paul Henri Holbach, toward religion, and their overall skepticism, "the strongest intellectual forces of the Enlightenment do not lie in its rejection of belief but rather in the new form of faith which it proclaims, and in the new form of religion which it embodies."[11]

On the other hand, no Ming neo-Confucianists ever publicly or even consciously rejected Confucian teaching. On the contrary, by explaining the world in accordance with the internal principle of their own minds instead of the external rules, radical disciples of Wang Yang-ming believed, in good faith, that they were the true loyal interpreters of Confucius's thought.

This belief, moreover, was not groundless, since Confucianism, like Christianity, does not exist as a single truth but in its various forms of interpretation. The novel, as a subversive form due to its use of a language closer to that of everyday life and its portrayal of ordinary people, exemplifies this ambiguous relationship between the object of transgression and the transgressive force in both French and Chinese cultures.

If the range of available choices in Chinese literature appears limited, eighteenth-century France seemingly presents a broader spectrum of works. It is true that the eighteenth-century French novel is not devoid of influence from works of the same genre in other European countries—such as the works of Cervantes, the picaresque novelists in Spain, and Samuel Richardson in Britain. The narrowly focused topic of the present study, however, makes it essential to restrict my corpus to one Western literature.

Since my study is mainly concerned with sexuality, which occupies a predominant position in the novelistic world, this ruled out the large corpus of the French "descendants" of the picaresque tradition.[12] In these works, the sexual life of the "picaro" remains in the background, subordinated to the need for survival and social ambition.[13] Furthermore, I have limited my study to two aspects of sexuality—perversion and sublimation.

In the first case, both the French libertine and the Chinese erotic master consciously use objects of desire as instruments of physical pleasure. In the second case, the worship of the beloved by the lover, the French romantics or the Chinese refined adolescents, requires a large degree of desexualization or symbolization of desire. This condition excludes works in which "lofty love" is mingled with "destructive and perverse desire," such as L'abbé Prevost's *Manon Lescaut* and *L'Histoire d'une Grecque moderne*.

In this case, if *Julie, ou la Nouvelle Héloïse* and *Les Liaisons dangereuses* are not the only novels of eighteenth-century France capable of meeting my criteria, they are at least among the most representative ones in their respective aspects. Furthermore, the intertextual relationship of the two French novels resembles that of the two Chinese novels—but in reverse. Laclos was a fervent reader of Rousseau, and his libertine novel seems, in many respects, to parody Rousseau's preromantic work.[14] Similarly, the author of *The Dream of the Red Chamber* consciously imitated *The Golden Lotus* in certain passages. Moreover, *The Dream of the Red*

Chamber owes a great deal to *The Golden Lotus* in its descriptions of a large household as a microcosm of society, as the latter is considered the most successful—if not the *only* successful—family drama among the former's predecessors.[15]

To a large extent, *Les Liaisons dangereuses* and *The Golden Lotus* treat the same aspect of sexuality—namely, the perverse search for gratification in sexual relations. On the one hand, Laclos's libertines, Valmont and Merteuil, by their antisocial complicity, convert the society around them into a playground. They are the players who wield psychological power to reduce the "honest people" to the status of playthings. On the other hand, Hsi-men Ch'ing, the lewd hero of *The Golden Lotus*, turns his large household into a scene of orgy, endlessly seeking the gratification of his immediate desire from his six wives and numerous lovers.

If eighteenth-century France was notorious for its license, sixteenth-century China also witnessed the emergence of a large number of erotic works in the forms of novel, drama, and painting. As Van Gulik points out, the Chinese erotic art of this period is characterized by a relative absence of "sadism,"[16] which may be considered an extreme form of libertinism, since both sadists and libertines derive their pleasure in part from a negation of the sense of guilt.

Although this pleasure can be expressed in flesh-and-blood realities, the shadow of God, demoniac as it is, is often present in the most cynical scenes of seduction in Laclos's libertine novel or in the most violent scenes in Sade's works. Christopher Lasch sees the emergence of sadism as a logical outcome of the undermining of religious and moral values in Western culture by the Enlightenment cult of rationality, practical reason, and the critical attitude.[17]

Libertinism or sadism is not only the by-product of this extreme form of rationality, but also the by-product of what this form claims to reject—namely, religious values. Needless to say, libertinism cannot exist outside of a Christian context because the subversive force is determined by the object of its subversion.[18]

In the Chinese novel, pleasure carries a more concrete undertone. Merteuil, Valmont, or Sadien heroes have to invent obstacles and torture their victims (either physically or psychologically) to "prove" their power in a positivist or "rational" way, whereas the power of the Chinese hero in relation to his partner is measurable by his sexual potency, his money, and his social position. In other words, the psychological power Laclos's characters enjoy consists of a well-structured self-image, whereas the power of the Chinese erotic master is "substantialized" by physical, economic, and social factors. This may explain in part why it would be much more difficult for a Chinese woman to play the dominant role in sexual game—as the Marquise de Merteuil does—since social power was one of the most male-oriented aspects in the past. Largely because of the overwhelmingly significant social power, the heroines in *The Golden Lotus* are mostly "playthings" instead of "players" in their games.

The "fortification"[19] of the self in Laclos's novel requires a self-control that is not so different from asceticism, as in the case of Scipio in Valmont's own comparison. The libertines' self-discipline differs from that of the moralists', not in form but in aim since Valmont and Merteuil use their self-control in order to reach the opposite end—the profanation of moral and religious values—more efficiently. In fact, as Merteuil states in her famous autobiographical letter, much of her libertine "training" is based on moral standards that she had to learn either from prudish people or from moralistic books. In a sense, Merteuil's "fortress of the self" is also a prison in which she willingly submits to the restrictions that she herself has imposed. Her law is no less strict than social law, and her freedom consists of choosing the rules according to her wish.

The "dispersal of the self" in the Chinese novel results from a lack of concern for the future. Hsi-men Ch'ing does not see any need to control his desire. On the contrary, he aims at the maximum gratification of his immediate desire, so that his life is composed by the images of contingent elements and the successive objects of desire, such as money, food, women, rank, wine, and the like. In Laclos's novel, financial concern is almost completely absent, whereas in *The Golden Lotus*, sex is always mingled with material self-interest. The Chinese novel, however, differs from the picaresque novel in the West, because these material elements alone cannot constitute the main object of desire for the hero, despite their overwhelming importance. From the point of view of the "player"—which means the *male* protagonist—these elements are either decoration or justification for sexual desire, and, for this reason, remain in the background. Generally speaking, the parvenu Hsi-men does not need to work harder for his money than most aristocrats. At the same time, pleasure and money for the protagonist of *The Golden Lotus* is always interchangeable, even if this were in Buddhist Paradise.[20]

The assumption that the conceptualization of sexual pleasure belongs to the Western culture seems from a different angle to confirm a commonly accepted notion described as "metaphysical desire" in Denis de Rougement's terms[21] and as "triangular desire" in René Girard's terms.[22] Indeed, libertinism is the reversal of *l'amour courtois*—or the outcome of its disillusion. Nevertheless, this does not mean necessarily that I try to simplify the problem by distributing "desire" to French libertines and "need" to the Chinese erotic master.[23] Even though the French and the Chinese protagonists express their desire in different forms—one is more abstract, and the other is more concrete—the result is not totally different. Hsi-men Ch'ing, at the end of the novel, also suffers from a void that cannot be filled even at the price of his life. In the end, the desire for material quantity is also a "metaphysical desire," since quantity is meaningless without qualitative distinction. The great number of short-term relationships reduces his numerous partners to a single pattern of women, so that his frantic activities constitute a mere gesture of repetition.

Very often Hsi-men seeks out a certain diversity in the shadow of a third person—the husband of his lover—which explains his relative indifference toward unmarried girls.[24] At the beginning, most of his lovers' husbands—who happen to be his servants—do not represent real obstacles. Even when they are not servants—as in the case of Wu Ta and Hua Tzu-hsü—they are weak and subject to Hsi-men's political power. With one or two exceptions, most of them are more than willing to "rent" their wives to the rich and powerful master in exchange for material benefits.

Before his death, a sense of lack grows stronger and stronger to the point that Hsi-men starts longing for more and more inaccessible women, such as wives of high officials or heirs of powerful families. Instead of trying to reach the "unreachable" as Valmont does in his relations with Tourvel, Hsi-men prefers to turn to the bodies of some servants to satisfy his craving. Valmont does the same thing with Cécile, while waiting for the capitulation of his "merciless devoted." Hsi-men, however, takes this substituted flesh seriously, whereas the French libertine considers his flirtation merely an entertainment. Psychologically burned out by his longing for the unreachable body, and physically exhausted by the surrogate lovers, Hsi-men literally dies of "dissemination." The symptom of the overflowing of excessive desire, the dispersal of semen, signifies the complete disintegration of the self.

The difference between the French libertines' conceptualization and the Chinese erotic master's concretization of desire is manifested through their different treatments of the rhetoric of love in the other pair of novels in this study. Rousseau's lovers show much more linguistic awareness in defining their love than Ts'ao Hsüeh-ch'in's adolescents. Nevertheless, *Julie, ou la Nouvelle Héloïse* and *The Dream of the Red Chamber* share a point in common: both are considered important works of love in their respective cultures.

First, Rousseau and Ts'ao Hsüeh-ch'in question the validity of the commonly accepted social principle according to which passion (or love)—an individual value—should submit itself to reason (or moral standards)—a trans-individual value, and both authors seem to show a preference for the former. This individual value, however, is "domesticated" by its object of substitution: the trans-individual value. The "sensitive soul" in Rousseau's work is sublime as long as it is led by reason, whereas the "essence" (*ch'i*)[k] of those Chinese lovers remains superior insofar as they maintain a sense of decorum.

Second, both works try to idealize the notion of love. In *Julie, ou la Nouvelle Héloïse*, sensuality is seen as corrupting love by plunging that noble feeling into an imperfect world of reality. In *The Dream of the Red Chamber*, any serious sensual experience between the two adolescent lovers is subtly avoided, not only because it might offend their sense of decorum, but also because it would smack too much of vulgar lovers, such as most of the hero's lustful male cousins.

Third, both the French and the Chinese authors adopt an aesthetic attitude that allows them to treat passion mainly as an object of contemplation, relatively free of ethical judgment. Since aesthetic judgment is mainly subjective, this shifting transcends social reality by individualizing collective ethics.

Despite their similar features, the means of sublimation, idealization, or aestheticization of passion remain very different in the French and the Chinese novels.

In *Julie, ou la Nouvelle Héloïse*, the sublimation of sexual desire is accomplished for the lovers by means of a process that seeks to substitute writing for the material object of passion and thereby to distance them from the present experience either spatially or temporally. Thus, they can only achieve happiness together by reconstituting their experience in such a way that the present must inevitably seem a misfortune in comparison with the narrative image of the past. That image is superior to actual experience, because it is committed to writing and is therefore immutable, whereas the present is empirical and thus open to alteration. The realization of passion is also fatal to its duration, since the world is always changing, whereas love is sublime because of its constancy. Only by loving the image of Julie, then, can St. Preux make his passion go beyond the vicissitudes of his worldly fortune.

Finally, the physical satisfaction of desire is also its elimination. Julie states in one of her letters that the essence of life lies in the act of desiring. What one desires is not necessarily a concrete object, since the desire that can be satisfied in this world is not higher than its object. The object worthy of desire is "illusion," as Julie says in *Julie, ou la Nouvelle Héloïse*. In this sense, writing is a form of "desire for desire," and fiction becomes higher than reality through its representation of illusion.

Ts'ao Hsüeh-ch'in seems to share the same point of view about the order of reality and illusion, since in *The Dream of the Red Chamber* fiction or the creation of the novel is considered as an experience more genuine than life itself.[25] Through a process of aestheticization, the "useless" tears are equivalent to the "useful" ink with which the author writes the novel. However, in Rousseau's novel, language functions as a substitute for the concrete object of love, which means that language is still considered as primarily representational—not necessarily as representing reality, but paradoxically as representing the reality of illusion, which is passion.

Therefore, love and its language dovetail to a far greater degree than do love and the world in Rousseau's novel, whereas in Ts'ao Hsüeh-ch'in's novel language is mostly inadequate to express feelings. This difference can be in part explained in the context of the Christian tradition, in which the language of love is interchangeable with religious language. In the *Song of Songs*, the expressions of sensual love are understood as the exaltation of love for God. In many Christian writings, such as St. Augustine's *Confessions*, religious emotion is expressed through erotic language. We can call this phenomenon "spiritual eroticism." In medieval literature, troubadours and writers of the chivalrous romances reversed "spiritual eroticism" and used religious language to spiritualize worldly love in the forms of "courtly love."[26] To a certain extent, this tradition facilitates the task of communication for the Western novelists and their characters. St. Preux and Julie often describe each other in biblical language, and Julie even justifies her passion for her love by identifying it with her devotion to God. Love expressed in such a language becomes the best part of the lover—provided that it can be separated from his or her physical longing.

In the Chinese context, the lack of a similar extensive rhetorical tradition makes the communication between lovers more difficult and also more interesting. This does not mean that China lacks a lyrical tradition, but rather the lyricism in China is not transcended by the same kind of mysticism through religious language as in the Western tradition. The fragrant-herb-and-beauty tradition created by Ch'ü Yüan is not similar to that of courtly love, because ruler-subject relations are still located in this world.

Ai-ch'ing,[1] the Chinese equivalent of the Western expression "love," is an invention of the late nineteenth century, possibly deriving from some translations of Western novels. *Ai*[m] etymologically means "to be stingy." In *The Golden Lotus, ai* is used to describe Hsi-men Ch'ing's fondness for one part of the body of a lover (legs, hands, skin, and so on). In other words, the expression in this context has mainly a physical implication.

In *The Dream of the Red Chamber,* "love" (*ai*), is used as a verb with concrete nouns, as in "caring for things" (*ai-wu*).[n] Occasionally, "vulgar" lovers may use this expression in their dirty jokes.

Chiao Pao-yü and Lin Tai-yü, however, never use the term *ai* to express their feelings to each other. "Sentiment" (*ch'ing*)[o], as a noun, is described as bordering on "excessiveness" or "lust" (*yin*)[p] by an important supernatural spokeswoman of the author, "the fairy of Disenchantment"[27] (*Ching-huan hsien-tzu*).[q]

In fact, Ch'in K'e-ch'ing, the character who personifies "sentiment" (*ch'ing*) by the double pun of her name, exemplifies this ambiguous nature of love. She is distinguished for both her beauty and intelligence. But this does not prevent her from having an incestuous relationship with her father-in-law. A verse describes Ch'in K'e-ch'ing in Pao-yü's dream: "Love, meeting with its like, breeds lust."[28] Like K'e-ch'ing's personality, love is a morally ambiguous finger.

Linguistically, there is no clear distinction between the spiritual and the physical, or between love and lust in this Chinese novel. In a sense, Pao-yü's "lust of intention" (*yi-yin*)[r] is more blameworthy than "the shallow vulgar lust of the flesh" (*p'i-fu lan-yin*)[s] of common people, because of the former's unusual and nonconformist nature. Moreover, since what is involved in the "lust of intention" is the mind, Pao-yü commits himself more deeply to lust than an ordinary lustful man.[29] At the same time, this lack of distinction between love and lust does not necessarily imply a condemnation of Pao-yü's love, since the fairy refers to the judgment of the common people at this point. Their opinion is very often contemptibly rejected by Pao-yü and his kind as superficial and nonsensical. Furthermore, their blame sometimes constitutes indirect but important praise of the hero's nonconformism and originality, thanks to the two different axiological systems between the garden and the real world.

The Garden of the Great View—in which Pao-yü grows up as the only male inhabitant among his innocent female cousins and young maids—has a different, if not opposite, value system. The fairy, whose "Land of Illusion" (*t'ai-hsü huan-ching*)[t] is considered by critics as a supernatural image of the garden,[30] defines the superiority of Pao-yü's love from an aesthetic point of view. According to her, a lustful man longs for a female beauty in order to satisfy his physical need of the moment, but Pao-yü's attachment to the girls in the garden consists mainly of a contemplative pleasure.

In other words, the common man uses female beauty as he uses food, clothes, and other everyday things, whereas Pao-yü admires it as he would a work of art—even though this contemplative pleasure may be associated with sexual acts.

What is at stake is the difference between an artist and a philistine; but the former is not necessarily morally superior to the latter. He is only more refined in an aesthetic sense. For lack of an appropriate vocabulary, the fairy can only define Pao-yü's feeling either by its very nature of indeterminacy—"it can be understood intuitively, but not communicated in language"—or by contrast—"it has different meaning from common lust."

Whereas Rousseau maintains a spatial distance between his two lovers or a temporal distance between the lovers and their experience of love, Ts'ao Hsüeh-ch'in separates his work from the real world by inserting the supernatural world and different layers of dream as the frameworks of the novelistic world. Pao-yü's garden is an illusory world within illusion, a land of dream within a dream. The illusion is the world and the dream is life. At a linguistic level, the author of *The Dream of the Red Chamber* deliberately disregards the semantic restrictions of certain expressions.

As we have seen, "lust" (*yin*), a pejorative term, acquires a positive connotation in the expression of "the lust of intention" (*yi-yin*). On other occasions, the expressions used by common people to criticize the hero—such as "crazy" (*k'uang*)[u] and "idiotic" (*sha*)[v]—are the very marks of his distinguished personality, which is beyond the understanding of the real world. Nevertheless, the distance between the garden and the world, or the divergence between idiosyncratic language and common language may ironically turn against the subjective world of the hero, since ultimately, reality destroys the idealistic world of the garden.

In any case, love cannot exist without language since it is, itself, largely a product of language. In *Julie, ou la Nouvelle Héloïse*, quotations from previous literary works ease the lovers' task of expressing their love, whereas in *The Dream of the Red Chamber*, quotations from romantic plays, such as *The Peony Pavilion*[31] (*moutan t'ing*),[w] become a source of the lovers' quarrels largely because love and lust are linguistically indistinguishable in this context. At the same time quarrels permit the lovers to understand each other's feelings much better.

Both lovers are, to a degree, disturbed by two contradictory needs: the desire to communicate their love and the contempt for a language traditionally associated with lust—especially in the case of Tai-yü—which is nevertheless indispensable to their communication. In other words, although the language used in the romantic drama may offend their sense of decorum, it remains nevertheless the language closest to their personal feelings, and it is only after they read some sentimental plays including *The Peony Pavilion* that they begin to understand themselves.

Paradoxically, misunderstanding is the only means which enables the two lovers to understand each other. Since the language they dispose of can express their feelings only obliquely, quarrels are the price they pay to adjust themselves to a new means of communication. Tedious efforts of arguing over a trivial expression help the lovers to invent a language more suitable to their feelings. Moreover, their quarrels confirm their mutual attachment in that each word of the speaker is taken seriously by the listener despite—or because of—its unsuccessful communication. If *The Dream of the Red Chamber* is considered *the* masterpiece of Chinese fiction, it is largely because it goes against the grain of a rhetoric of sexual relations that prevails in traditional Chinese narrative. In this case, we can agree with Harold Bloom: the breaking of a form becomes its more successful manifestation.[32]

1

Libertinism: A Form of Structuring the Self

Les *Liaisons dangereuses*[1], the eighteenth-century French libertine novel and *The Golden Lotus*,[2] the Chinese erotic novel of the sixteenth century, share one point in common: the perverse attitude of their heroes toward sexual relations. Despite the similarity, however, the two works are strikingly different in the manners in which their respective protagonists pursue their perverse measures.

In the Chinese novel, the self of the erotic hero is materialized by and dispersed into numerous objects of desire. The dispersal of the self leads to a collapse of the family, which is, at the same time, a destruction of the country since, in the Confucian tradition, the individual, the family, and society form a chain of mutual dependency.[3] By contrast, Laclos's novel, written in 1782, bears the mark of its century in its idolatrous portrayal of knowledge and reason in the form of the pursuit of psychological power that can be wielded in the perverse game of love.

This may in part explain the difference between the "libertine fortress"[4] in the case of the French libertines and the dispersal of the self in the case of the Chinese erotic master. The "fortification of the self" is motivated not only by the intellectual ambience of the century of Enlightenment, but also by the heritage of the Christian tradition itself as the object of its transgression. The human soul is supposed to be the "glass" through which one "sees darkly" the image of God.[5] The search for a transcendent self becomes the way of seeking the image of God, as in St. Augustine's *Confessions*. Romanticism "naturalizes"—to borrow Meyer Abrams's expression—this supernatural version of the self by substituting a creative individual or a sensitive soul for the image of God.[6]

Laclos's libertine heroes react against Rousseau's romantic heroes. Their pleasures derives not only from profaning the notion of a transcendent self but especially its humanized version. The Marquise de Merteuil and the Vicomte de Valmont try to assume a godlike position in the hearts of their victims, mocking all sentimental values and the human relationships of friendship, love, family ties, marriage, and the like. But in doing so, they risk being contaminated by these values, as in the relationship of Valmont with Tourvel.

Moreover, their world of the self is determined by its own object of parody—namely, the romantic or preromantic self. Therefore, it is not an exaggeration to say that Laclos's libertines are the mirror images of Rousseau's romantic lovers. Some critics consider Merteuil an anti-Héloïse and Valmont an anti-St. Preux.[7] Indeed, they remain, nonetheless, the sister and brother of Rousseau's heroes—perverse as they are.

Pleasure of Knowledge, Pleasure of Power

Joan DeJean was right in her definition of the Marquise de Merteuil's subjectivity as a "libertine fortress," because not physical pleasure but rather the pleasure of power acquired through her superior knowledge and intelligence is what motivates her in her game. Pleasure and power become interchangeable, as Malraux has shown.[8] She is a creature of the century of Enlightenment, despite the author's claim to the contrary in the

"Publisher's Note."[9] In fact, the knowledge and art of hypocrisy are complementary, since for Merteuil, the one most powerful is that individual who knows the most but is the least known.

In letter 141, the Marquise de Merteuil reproaches Valmont for being unable to become the lover or the friend of a woman: "never a woman's lover or friend, but always her tyrant or her slave" (4:141:310). In a metaphor Merteuil uses frequently, she compares the Vicomte to a sultan, the Présidente to his favorite sultana. At the beginning of the novel, in order to entice Valmont back from the countryside where he has lingered too long near his devout Tourvel, Merteuil describes her erotic experience with the Chevalier:

> I pleased myself by considering him as a Sultan in the midst of a harem in which I was successively the different favorites. (1:10:22)

Later on, when Valmont insists on renewing their past relationship, Merteuil answers:

> I may sometimes have claimed to take the place of a harem by myself, but it has never suited me to be part of one. (4:127:283)

In fact, Merteuil herself interprets sexual relationship in the same terms—namely, as the relationship between master and slave. The only difference is that she wants to reverse the roles of sultan and sultana. By herself constituting the entire harem of the chevalier, she actually becomes his sultan: she is everything he may desire, but he is only one of her objects of desire.

This reversal, instead of changing the rules of a male dominant society—such as those of harem—only reinforces them by playfully exchanging sexual roles. According to Merteuil, a woman who plays the role of sultan must be a merciless tyrant, precisely because she cannot expect any merciful treatment from the society.

Libertinism is thus a game through which Merteuil acquires the freedom of tyrannizing others. Devoid of any practical aim, this game is ludicrous. But, at the same time, it is serious in its mercilessness, as in her rivalry with the Présidente de Tourvel. The value of another human being for Merteuil lies only in his or her function in this game: Is that person useful or harmful to the player? The society around her is nothing more than a drama in which everyone exists only to play a role as the object of her exercise of power. The Marquise writes in letter 81 about her late husband:

> He died, as you know, shortly afterward; and although, taking it all round, I had no reason to complain of him, I felt none the less keenly the value of the liberty my widowhood would give me and I promised myself to make good use of it. (2:81:163)

She views him dispassionately with neither hatred nor love, but only as a potential restraint of her so-called freedom—that is, family ties, friendship, love and in short, all human affections—are reduced to and also serve to camouflage a utilitarian relationship of power.

To a certain extent, this position is justifiable in that widowhood would have afforded the only possible freedom for a woman who lives under the authority of her father before marriage and under the authority of her husband afterward. Only after the death of her husband can she be herself to enjoy financial and personal freedom.

The free and independent widow is also a common figure in Pierre Marivaux's plays.[10] Nevertheless, Merteuil's matter-of-fact tone in describing the death of her husband remains striking, since this emotionless attitude is also dominant in her relationship with any other person. Because she does not allow any emotion to disturb her reason, she can win battles as a mathematic genius in her infallible calculations. Moreover, depriving herself of most sentiments of ordinary people, she plays the role of an impassible divinity. The only emotion that is left, besides the pleasure of power, is anger. This emotion, which divinities seem to share with human beings without too much difficulty, is the cause of the Marquise's downfall at the end of the book.

The Marquise indeed compares herself with God from time to time, as the following passage shows us:

> At my waking, I found two notes, one from the mother and one from the daughter; I could not keep from laughing when I found literally the same phrase in both: "It is from

you alone I expect any consolation." Is it not indeed amusing to console for and against, and to be the only agent of two directly opposite interests? Here I am like the Divinity, receiving the contrary prayers of blind mortals and changing nothing in my immutable decrees. (2:63:115)

Just as between God and his believers there may not be any equality, so between the player and her plaything. To this extent, the idolatry of a lover is less satisfactory than the blind trust of someone who has the illusion of being her friend. A stupid lover still expects a concrete proof—such as physical pleasure—whereas a stupid friend does not expect anything else but advice. The fact that physical pleasure has to be shared implies a limited equality, whereas the so-called friendship can be based merely on illusion.

However sincere the praise of a lover may be, it may, nevertheless, be used as a means of exchange for sexual favor. The advice that Cécile and her mother expect from the Marquise facilitates her power game. The desire for her advice is equal to the implicit recognition of Merteuil's absolute power, because the trust of these "mortals" is "blind," and based on complete ignorance of their omniscient master. Both of them are victims of a situation created by Merteuil, whom they paradoxically take to be their savior.

The mutual mistrust between the two closely related persons, mother and daughter, sets off their common "blind" faith in the one who is their true enemy. Moreover, at the linguistic level, the unconscious repetition of the same formula further confirms the religious nature of this "faith": like a prayer, it is repeated by various believers.

In this situation, Merteuil derives absolute power from her monopoly on knowledge. The master, in other words, is the one who knows, and the slave is the one who remains ignorant. Conversely, the master is the one who does not let others know himself or herself, whereas the slave is the one who is easily known by others. For this reason, Merteuil prefers hypocrisy to honesty: since a powerful person is the one who possesses others by his superiority of knowledge, a hypocrite is in a better position to safeguard this superiority.

According to Merteuil, no one is truly sincere. That people believe they are sincere, she contends, is based more on their own illusions than on tangible facts. Because the fundamental truth of the society is the discrepancy between "being" and "appearance," sincerity can result only from a misinterpretation of this fact, or from the art of self-deception. Thus, the critical issue is not how to distinguish between sincerity and hypocrisy, but rather how to take advantage of the self-deception of those allegedly sincere people in order to exploit their ignorance. The honest people are "the fools" "for our tiny pleasures"—as Merteuil and Valmont say, quoting Gresset. (2:63:124)

Merteuil, for example, can exploit Mme. Volanges's vanity to keep secret the Marquise's pretended confession to Volanges's own daughter because the latter "wishes to impress her daughter with her own acuteness." (2:62:123) As Merteuil sees it, people who seek to attain a reputation that is undeserved are liars. Needless to say, Merteuil does not give any credit to virtue, since women who "claim merit and virtue since they can have no pretension to charm" (2:81:164) merely provide another example of self-deception for her.

In the final analysis, everyone is a liar, and there is no socially significant distinction between truth and falsehood. There is only a distinction between cleverness and stupidity: some people are aware that they are lying and try to take advantage of this fact, whereas others lie unconsciously and to no purpose. The divergence between "appearance" and "being" within the society forces everyone to lie in one way or another, willingly or not.

According to the Marquise, it is better to be a liar who assumes responsibility for his or her lies than to be an alleged sincere person who lies at random and unconsciously. Ultimate truth, then, is nothing else but power acquired through knowledge. Understanding the subjective nature of truth constitutes a major part of this knowledge. Furthermore, the obtuseness of the common people justifies their roles as "playthings" in Merteuil's game: they fall into her traps because they are, first of all, the victims of their own illusions.

Although Valmont represents for Merteuil a different category of people—that is, those who understand this reality—she still considers herself to be superior. Concerning the trap set for Prévan, a libertine like Valmont, she writes in letter 85:

> How convenient it is to have to deal with you "men of principles!" Sometimes a bungling lover disconcerts one by his timidity or embarrasses one by his passionate raptures; it is a fever which, like others, has its cold shiverings and its burning, and sometimes varies in its symptoms. But it is so easy to guess your prearranged advance! The arrival, the bearing, the tone, the remarks—I knew what they would all be the evening before. (2:85:178)

The "men of principle" are different from ordinary people because they realize the nullity of the social rules that guide the behavior of the common people. On this point, they share a common ground with the Marquise de Merteuil. Nevertheless, if they scorn the common people who blindly believe in the social code, their actions are no less "coded"; and their code, though less familiar, cannot sustain a claim to freedom and creative imagination either.

Their understanding of the divergence between "being" and "appearance" in society puts them at an advantage in comparison with the common people, but, in Merteuil's opinion, they remain students, not masters of this knowledge. They follow the rules set up by others and do not base their actions mainly on their own observations as the Marquise does. In this sense, they also follow a code blindly.

Merteuil, however, has no choice but to invent most of her principles, for it requires much more resourcefulness for a woman—who has fewer role models—to play the role of a libertine than a man.

According to Merteuil, this is the major difference between herself and male libertines. As they are mastered by their knowledge of "libertine principles," she, by contrast, is the master of the same knowledge. She can shake their power through her knowledge of their principles; yet she can still prevent them from shaking hers since her principles, based as they are on her own observations, are less predictable and less susceptible to appropriation. Because the position of women forces her to invent new rules if she wants to join the libertine game set up in accordance with men's rules, Merteuil becomes the champion in this game. The invention of new rules enables her to be unpredictable—and thus more powerful—than others in this game of knowledge and power.

Contrary to what the author states in the so-called "Publisher's Note,"[11] the valorization of knowledge based on one's own understanding makes the Marquise a person well adapted to the milieu of an aspect of the Enlightenment. As Christopher Lasch writes about Sade's "sexual utopia":

> In a society that has reduced reason to mere calculation, reason can impose no limits on the pursuit of pleasure—on the immediate gratification of every desire no matter how perverse, insane, criminal, or merely immoral. For the standards that would condemn crime or cruelty derive from religion, compassion, or the kind of reason that rejects purely instrumental applications; and none of these outmoded forms of thought or feeling has any logical place in a society based on commodity production. In his misogyny, Sade perceived that bourgeois enlightenment, carried to its logical conclusions, condemned even the sentimental cult of womanhood and the family; which the bourgeois itself had carried to unprecedented extremes.[12]

The cult of knowledge necessarily undermines the worship of God or of any kind of authority, religious or ethical: knowing can only begin with questions, whereas the nature of authority is to be unquestionable. To question an authority is to doubt or even to deny its validity. In the end, what replaces ethical or religious authority is the authority of interest, or a commodified reason as an instrument with which one acquires power, as in the Marquise's case. In fact, Merteuil is like a Sadian character in that her acquisition of knowledge carries her to one of the "logical conclusion" of the "bourgeois enlightenment": everything is permitted.

As she states, "I did not desire to enjoy, I wanted to know; my desire to learn suggested the means to me". (2:81:162) Any "means" must be good, if they satisfy her "desire to learn," because a commodity is not judged in accordance with its moral value, but with its exchange value.

To this extent, her utilitarianism even in the unpractical world of aristocracy remains more bourgeois than the sentimental revery of Tourvel, whom most critics since Baudelaire consider the representative of the bourgeoisie par excellence.[13] As the old lady Rosemonde reminds us in her letter to Tourvel, "I notice it because I recollect that was always the style of love. I see it is now as it used to be." (3:103:222) On the other hand, Merteuil "rarely listens to anything of this kind which is not a topic of the day." (2:74:137)

In this sense, Tourvel belongs to an almost vanished past; Merteuil belongs to the present. The devout *présidente* bases her behavior on religious and ethical principles, whereas the Machiavellian Marquise uses her reason only for "instrumental applications."

According to Nobert Elias, ever since Louis XIV, the aristocracy has been "contaminated" by the value system of the bourgeoisie, which in its turn imitated courtly society.[14] Rationality, usually attributed to the bourgeoisie as its exclusive property, becomes the central value that dominates the aristocratic society of Laclos's libertine novel. Indeed, Merteuil believes that the difference between herself and a good politician of her time is merely superficial. Instead of developing her talent on the political stage with the objective of acquiring social power, she uses it to explore the battlefield of the libertine game with the objective of achieving psychological domination. In short, one can say that her personality captures best the spirit of her time.

> I was not yet fifteen and already I possessed the talents to which the greater part of our politicians owe their reputation; and I considered myself still in the first elements of the science I wished to acquire. (2:81:162)

Merteuil must be stronger than anyone else in this game of power, because the game is, supposedly the exclusive propriety of men. Even though she claims to be born "to avenge my sex and to dominate yours," (2:81:160), in no way does this mean that she is interested in defending the interests of her sex or that her thinking anticipates feminism as several critics, such as Anne-Marie Jaton,[15] believe.

To "avenge her sex" for the Marquise means to excel in the art of living in a male-dominant world in accordance with their rules of domination and power. She wants to be the master of men as well as of women. As a matter of fact, being a woman is accidental for Merteuil. The fact that her sex is supposed to be weaker is merely additional proof of her personal merit, for a woman who plays the game of love must necessarily be superior.

> As to prudence and shrewdness, I do not mention myself— but where is the woman who would not possess more than you? . . . Believe me, Vicomte, people rarely acquire the qualities they can dispense with. You fought without risk and acted without wariness. For you men, defeats are simply so many victories the less. In this unequal struggle our fortune is not to lose and your misfortune not to win. If I granted you as many talents as we have, still how much we should surpass you from the continual necessity we have of using them! (2:81:159)

This judicious observation is not so much a protestation against the inequality of the sexes as an expression of Merteuil's self-admiration. If for a woman "not to lose" carries as much merit as does the victory for a man, what should be the merit of a woman who always prevails over her male partners, including the best of them: the Vicomte de Valmont?

However, the inequality of sexes is the motivation for the Marquise's self-training. Her training is modeled upon male examples, because she wants, not only to surpass the opposite sex in this libertine game, but also to become different from her own sex. Indeed, the more she excels in this game, the more she distinguishes herself from her own sex. In fact, other women are merely counterexamples of her superior image. The Vicomte also implicitly acknowledges her superiority by writing the following sentences:

> I do not think I am more stupid than others. I have found a hundred, I have found a thousand ways of dishonoring a woman; but when I have tried to find a way to save her from dishonor, I have never found the possibility of it. (2:76:141)

Although he qualifies this statement by adding that Merteuil's victory is due more to her luck than to her skill, he recognizes that his role is a "hundred" times, if not a "thousand" times, easier than Merteuil's. Valmont's warning later on prompts the Marquise to write her famous autobiographical letter. In her assessment, she has completely reversed the situation by virtue of her "finesse" and "prudence" in order to achieve what Valmont considers as beyond his possibility:

> If you have seen me directing events and opinions and making these formidable men the toys of my caprices or my fantasies; depriving some of will, others of the power of harming me; if in accordance with my changing tastes I have turn by turn attached to my train or cast far from me "those enthroned tyrants now become my slaves;" if through these frequent revolutions I have kept my reputation intact; ought you not to have concluded that, since I was born to avenge my sex and to dominate yours, I must have created methods unknown to anybody but myself? (2:81:160)

"Toy" (*jouet*) signifies a passive object of pleasure that abandons itself utterly to an external force. In this sense, Merteuil presents herself as God, who manipulates human fate according to her "caprices" or "fantasies" without any rational explanation to her "toy." In "dethroning" men, Merteuil overturns the social order that bestows on them an unjustifiable and arbitrary superiority over women, and creates a new social hierarchy. She alone controls the fates of these men who normally tyrannize over the other sex; they are reduced to slaves by her superior intelligence.

Wicked as it is, her new order is supposedly more "rational," since it is based on personal talent and capacity. At the same time, it mirrors the order that it replaces in terms of its arbitrary and tyrannical nature. To "dethrone men" is also an act of castration: these men are reduced to roles traditionally assigned to women. Furthermore, they are deprived of language, as well as of their "puissance," because their secrets, as mastered by Merteuil, force them into silence on her own secret life—thus into "impuissance."

In this sense, sexual power is identified with power of speech. Put another way, it depends on "who has the voice." Indeed, the Marquise wins her battles often by discrediting "the voice" of her opponents.

By contrast, in the Chinese erotic novel, *The Golden Lotus*, sexual power is much more closely associated with social position. Since social power in the past was, in most cases, an exclusive propriety of men, it is much harder for P'an Chin-lien or any other female characters to play dominant roles as Merteuil does.

To a large extent, this "sexual" power which is reinforced by "textual" power must also be articulated in order to intensify its pleasure. In other words, sexual pleasure is also textual. The Marquise de Merteuil, for example, compares herself to a hero or a heroine of the past. Unlike Valmont, who makes a similar comparison in order to intensify the dramatic effect of his action, Merteuil's comparison emphasizes her position of power: she is superior not only to her contemporaries but also to her mythic predecessors in regard to the manipulation of power.

> Like a new Delilah I always used my power as she did to surprise this important secret. Ah! How many of our modern Samsons are there whose hair I keep under my scissors! (2:81:166)

Whereas Delilah learned the secret of one Samson, she, Merteuil, holds the secrets of a great number of "modern Samsons." Moreover, whereas in the Bible, Delilah actually cuts Samson's hair to accomplish an act of revenge, the Marquise needs only "to keep the hair under her scissors"—thereby prolonging and reinforcing the power and control that she enjoys over her lovers. One woman acted in reaction to the actual situation; the other "produces" a new situation by her performance. Moreover, the "modern Delilah" outdistances the ancient one in terms of both the duration and the intensity of the power.

Divinity of Opera

Whereas the Marquise de Merteuil actually *is* the libertine who seeks to dominate the battlefield of love affairs, the Vicomte de Valmont only *plays* the role of libertine: his world is a dramatic spectacle.

Not only is he a leading actor, but he is also the most important spectator. Moreover he is also the director who induces his victims, such as the Présidente de Tourvel, to act out his script. His scenario, or his libertine project, consists of mastering "time," which, in Poulet's terms, becomes a metaphor for the objective world. In other words, he would like to control the future for himself and his selected victims.[16] However, by lingering to admire his own performance, Valmont ends up being mastered by "time." To a degree, the passion for aesthetic enjoyment transforms the player of love into its plaything—just like his victims— since he is no longer only the master of the others' passion, but also the slave to his own passion.

Valmont is his own best audience. He is thoroughly impressed by his own performance as, on one occasion, when he returned unexpectedly to the house of his old aunt:

> In fact, I dropped from the sky like a Divinity at the Opera, who comes to wind up the plot. (2:76:152)

Unlike Merteuil who wants to equal divinity with her psychological power, Valmont is more interested in playing a dramatic god. In this case, the division of traditional sexual roles between man and woman is reversed in their libertine game. Whereas Merteuil has become a hard-working "professional," Valmont lingers in his aesthetic pleasure. As Roger Laufer points out, Valmont and Merteuil both try to succeed by using the means usually employed by the opposite sex: "The masterpiece of the woman tends toward pure action; that of the man sinks into the depth of life experience."[17]

This reversal of roles is also motivated by the special situation of their sexes. Merteuil explains to Valmont:

> For my own part, I must confess that one of the things which most flatters me is a sharp and well-conducted attack; where everything is carried out with order but with rapidity; which never puts us to the painful embarrassment of having ourselves to repair an awkwardness by which we ought to have profited; which preserves an air of violence even in those things we grant, and cunningly flatters our two favorite passions—the glory of defense and the pleasure of defeat. (1:10:9)

To a large extent, libertinism for Merteuil is not a game, but a war. Since a woman has to gamble on her reputation if she wants to join this game which is mainly reserved for the opposite sex, she must act with efficiency. In other words, a woman libertine is not only an ordinary player, but also a warrior. Needless to say, she must use the same means which her opposite sex normally uses in the war.

Indeed, unlike Merteuil, the Vicomte does not even consider the game as a "profession" since it is so easy for him. Libertinism is his hobby, his pastime. It is not surprising, therefore, that he adopts the attitude of his opposite sex toward life, since women in his class did not have any serious occupations. This difference is reflected in the writing styles of the two libertines. The Marquise's style is concise, precise, and sarcastic; the Vicomte's is precious, exaggerating, and sometimes ironically sentimental.

The two differ in other ways. For Merteuil, love is an illusion in which she cannot indulge: it could ruin her libertine career and her reputation. "It was there that I made certain that love, which they tell us is the cause of our pleasures, is, at most, only the pretext for them." (2:81:163)

Valmont, on the contrary, understands the illusory nature of love perfectly well, and thrives on it. Without it, victory is too simple, hence meaningless. Because he does not believe in love, to act as a lover is more challenging, thus more exciting.

> A woman's fairest moment, the only one in which she can produce that intoxication of the soul, which is always talked of and so rarely experienced, is the moment when we are certain of her love but not of her favors; (1:44:84)

In other words, the "fairest moment" is also the moment of illusion maintained by hope. Once obtained, the object of desire is no longer embellished by illusion and loses its values. In this sense, Valmont is not so remote from Rousseau's preromantic lovers. The difference is that the Vicomte lucidly "cultivates" his illusion to enhance his enjoyment of the game, whereas Julie and St. Preux are intoxicated with the superiority of illusion over reality.

Illusion, further, adds interest to life: "What! Do you think that very spectacle which makes you rush eagerly to the theatre, which you applaud there wildly is less interesting in reality?" (3:96:199). The Vicomte sinks so well into illusion that, in the end, he almost becomes a victim of his own "work" (*oeuvre*)—Tourvel. In fact, he is not completely deceptive in calling his so-called love for the Présidente "her work," (1:35:63) because he ends up identifying his libertine self on an existential level with his role of passionate lover on an aesthetic level.

> Indeed, if to be in love is not to be able to live without possessing that person one desires, to sacrifice to her one's time, one's pleasures, one's life; then I am really in love. (1:15:28)

Valmont, however, differs from someonc "really in love" (*réellement amoureux*) in that he is always the spectator, watching his own performance carefully and judging himself in the place of other spectators.

Sometimes, Valmont plays so seriously a role that it is even difficult for himself to tell whether his feeling has become identical to that of his role. For example, in order to win favor with Présidente de Tourvel, he, on one occasion, plays the role of philanthropist to save a peasant family from bankruptcy. He describes the impression that he has made on these people in a theatrical way:

> In the midst of the wordy benedictions of this family I was not unlike the hero of a play in the last scene. (1:21:38)

In whose eyes does he look like the "hero of a play"? Not necessarily in the eyes of those peasants, who take too seriously his good action to compare the scene with a drama. Not even in the eyes of the devoted Tourvel, who observes him through a servant charged with spying on the beloved libertine. She loves him too much to take this wonderful action as merely a performance.

It is rather in his own eyes that he is perceived as such. In other words, acting for him is not only a performance but also an entertainment. He enjoys and appreciates his own performance as a refined and cultivated spectator. The pleasure of watching intensifies the pleasure of action:

> My eyes filled with tears and I felt an involuntary but delicious emotion. (1:21:38)

Paradoxically, the intended cheater feels genuine emotion for his "good" deed, because the feeling caused by his successful cheating is "delicious." The distinction between a "philanthropist" and a "cheater" is blurred. So is the distinction between a lover and a libertine.

The same thing happens once to Hsi-men Ch'ing, the protagonist of *The Golden Lotus*. Like Valmont, Hsi-men also wants to exchange money for favor—not from his lover, but from Buddhas. Since he claims he would be able to buy sexual favor from all the divine beauties if he is willing to spend his propriety, he does not feel the need to disguise his exchange. As a result, he intends to remain cynically greedy and lustful even before any divinities. On this point, Hsi-men differs from his French counterpart in that the former has never thought about playing the role of the sincere lover.

One of the Vicomte's favorite roles is the lover *à la Saint Preux*, the hero of Rousseau's novel, who provides him with both the strategy of seduction and the object of parody. As the tender St. Preux tries to convince Julie of his feeling by referring to her own heart as the guarantee,[18] the libertine Valmont writes to Tourvel, the selected victim of his art of seduction:

> Well, I have one guarantee to offer you which you at least will not suspect: it is yourself. I only ask you to question yourself in good faith; if you do not believe in my love, if you doubt one moment that you alone reign over my soul, if you are not certain that you have attached this heart, which indeed has hitherto been but too fickle, I consent to bear the pain of this error. (2:52:98)

But St. Preux's argument is based on similarity between the two lovers, whereas in Valmont's case, the similarity is only a false appearance that masks the fundamental difference. The Présidente's "good faith" (*bonne foi*) enables the Vicomte's trick to succeed. In this sense, Tourvel herself becomes truly the "guarantee" (*garant*) not of sincere love, but of Valmont's successful acting.

Behind this irony lies a fundamental truth in this novel: the illusion or self-deception of allegedly sincere people is, in fact, what guarantees the success of the libertine trap. Or, the best way to corrupt an innocent person is, indeed, to confirm his or her illusion. In the end, Tourvel's good faith makes her believe in Valmont's acting so completely that she trusts him as much as Julie trusts St. Preux. As she writes to Mme. Rosemonde:

> Who knows whether we were not born for each other!
> (4:132:293)

At the same time, this belief is not necessarily wrong, since she is the perfect actress for Valmont's scenario. Moreover, their performance is so perfect that Valmont is contaminated by his role as a romantic lover. In the end, truth and acting is no longer distinguishable. In other words, the trap set by Valmont traps not only the game but also the hunter.

Very often Valmont himself needs illusion: he attributes to his spectators those reactions that he wishes to elicit from them. For example, he writes to Merteuil imagining his future victory over Tourvel's resistance:

> You yourself, my fair friend, will be seized by a holy respect and you will say enthusiastically: "Here is a man after my own heart." (1:4:8)

No one truly understands how Merteuil can believe this, since she can hardly praise anyone "enthusiastically" (*avec enthousiasme*) much less be "seized by a holy respect" (*saisie d'un saint repect*)—especially for Valmont's successful conquest of Tourvel's "tender" heart. Nevertheless, this sentence provides the Vicomte with a self-image which is "deliciously" satisfactory.

By using this expression with its religious connotations, Valmont no doubt has in mind his "tender devoted." Thus, by virtue of this displacement, he imagines that he gains a certain control over both Merteuil and her rival Tourvel, the two women he most eagerly desires to possess. He affords himself the aesthetic pleasure of having his possessions in a fictional situation.

This dramatization of power is more playful than the Marquise's search for psychological superiority. Where Merteuil relies more on the artful manipulation of her victims, her partner relies more on the opinion of his audience.

At first glance, the Marquise's psychological power seems more substantial than the Vicomte's dramatic effect. But in reality, the Vicomte can safely assume an attitude of detachment by identifying his spectators with himself, whereas the reality of the Marquise's supreme power depends upon the recognition of her potential rival. To this extent, one may say that Valmont plays a more self-sufficient role in the game than does Merteuil. This is determined by the different positions of their sexes in society.

The man can be publicly admired and also accepted in society for his skill in playing the libertine game. Even a prudish woman like de Volanges cannot close her door to him. (1:32:56) The woman, on the contrary, must hide her skill in order to maintain her respectability. The world is a stage for Valmont, since he can welcome other spectators besides himself. The Marquise can have only a single spectator in whom she has a little trust: Valmont.

The relationship between Merteuil and her only "connoisseur" belongs, by its very nature, to the category of the *"liaisons dangereuses,"* since a woman has no right to "show" her libertine skill on the stage of society. This relationship—antisocial as it is—nonetheless constitutes a social tie. It is more dangerous because of the Marquise's total dependency on Valmont's recognition. The Vicomte is completely secure within the confines of the game; only outside of it is his security threatened. The weapon that the Marquise uses against him at the end—politics—is not concerned with his private life but exclusively with his public life.

Valmont directs and coaches all the performance—his own and also of that of others, especially that of Tourvel. If she is the ideal victim and the perfect actress, it is, first of all, because of her reputation for invulnerable virtue:

> If they prefer the heroic, I shall point to Madame de Tourvel, that often quoted model of all the virtues! Respected

even by our greatest libertines! To such an extent that they had even abandoned the mere idea of attacking her! (3:115:254)

The gesture of singling out Tourvel allows Valmont to "show" his victory—for its dramatic effect. It is precisely this "sacredness" of Tourvel's virtue that arouses that most intense desire to profane it. As Valmont explains in letter 96:

Yes, I like to see, to watch this prudent woman impelled, without her perceiving it, upon a path which allows no return, and whose steep and dangerous incline carries her on in spite of herself, and forces her to follow me. There, terrified by the peril she runs, she would like to halt and cannot check herself. Her exertions and her skill may render her steps shorter; but they must follow one upon the other. Sometimes, not daring to look the danger in the face, she shuts her eyes, lets herself go, and abandons herself to my charge. More often her efforts are revived by a new fear; in her mortal terror she would like to try to turn back once again; she distances herself and very soon a magic power replaces her nearer the danger from which she had vainly tried to fly. Then having no one but me for guide and for support, without thinking of reproaching me for the inevitable fall, she implores me to retard it. Fervent prayers, humble supplications, all that mortals in their fear offer to the divinity, I receive from her; and you expect me to be deaf to her prayers, to destroy myself the worship she gives me, and rouse in casting her down that power she invokes for her support! Ah! At least leave me the time to watch these touching struggles between love and virtue. (3:96:198–99)

The more time-consuming the conquest, the more intense the aesthetic enjoyment. In this passage, Valmont uses verbs that describe a vision: "see" (*voir*), "consider" (*considérer*), and "observe" (*observer*) for describing the Présidente's mind. By visualizing Tourvel's fall, he makes it a "spectacle" of a psychological state.

The "new method" used by the Vicomte is more than a necessity, it is an object of contemplation in its own right. On the one hand, it vanquishes Tourvel's reputation for inflexible virtue; on the other hand, it makes of her an actress whose inner struggle becomes an exciting spectacle presented for her seducer.

Certain of the "end" (*dénouement*), the final success, Valmont, the director, can watch this struggle with a detached aesthetic pleasure, since his scenario is based on his "method." Tourvel must follow the "path" (*sentier*) that leads to the "inevitable fall" (*chute inévitable*), a route mapped out by her director.

As Laurent Versini points out in his notes in Laclos's *Oeuvres Complètes*, the libertine uses the language of a preacher. In this case, Valmont makes the devout Tourvel play the role of Julie in *La Nouvelle Héloïse*. Like Julie with regard to St. Preux, Tourvel, as a preacher might, would like to convert Valmont. Thus Valmont consciously plays the role of St. Preux, as Tourvel unconsciously identifies herself with Julie. The difference between the two actors is that the Présidente is ignorant of the true nature of their relationship: that is, as a romantic drama, not a romantic love.

By virtue of this discrepancy of knowledge, Valmont is the director—the master—and Tourvel is essentially the passive actress—the victim. For this reason the sincere prayer of the devout Tourvel (the substitute for Julie) addressed to Valmont (the fake St. Preux) does not serve to avert the fall but rather to make it inevitable. But, at the same time, it also postpones the "fall" and thereby prolongs Valmont's visual pleasure.

> Ah! The time will come too soon when, degraded by her fall, she will be nothing but an ordinary woman to me. (3:96:199)

Whether she *is* extraordinary or ordinary is not an important issue for Valmont, since he is more interested in her "performance" than in her person. Her performance is the image of his power—or the image of his self—because his subjective world is mainly based on the reaction of the outside world to his power game.

A show depends upon the reaction of its audience. Valmont's subjective world is, to a large degree, a long drawn-out drama, ever in search of theatrical effect. That is probably why

Merteuil says that she is her own "work" (*oeuvre*), whereas the "work" of Valmont is someone else, more precisely Mme. de Tourvel. The former would like to be unique in her "work," whereas the latter seeks uniqueness in his effects on others.

> Once I have achieved this triumph, I shall say to my rivals: "Behold my work, and seek a second example in the age!" (3:115:255)

Not only does Valmont play the lover to his victim in order to seduce her, but he also plays the role of libertine in the eyes of others to save his vanity from the ridicule of becoming a sincere lover. At the beginning he prefers to talk about Tourvel's uniqueness and, in so doing, justifies his choice. He replies to Merteuil's objection:

> Does Madame de Tourvel need illusion? No, she needs but to be herself and she is adorable. You censure her for dressing badly and I agree with you; all clothes do her injustice, whatever hides her disfigures her. In the unconstrained of her morning-dress she is indeed delightful. (1:4:12)

In this portrait of Tourvel, Valmont projects both what he desires for himself (self-sufficiency) as well as what is missing in his personality (being natural and sincere). "Unconstrained," the Présidente's quality of naturalness, is the very opposite of his libertine principle. To use Poulet's expression, Valmont's project is "the will to substitute for the indeterminate future, which is the work of chance, another predetermined future, which is the work of will."[19] It is his admiration of the quality that is precisely the opposite of his project, and unconsciously this becomes the point of departure for the betrayal of his principle. The libertine principle is, in fact, at odds with his aesthetic enjoyment, since his pleasure is rooted not in action but in watching himself acting. Thus, gradually, Valmont gives up his will to control the self and the world while indulging in an "unconstrained" pleasure, which is primarily aesthetic. Thereby, he, little by little and unconsciously, submits his well-structured subjective world to chance.

By a process of identification, Valmont gains the pleasure of admiring himself in his so-called "work," the Présidente de Tourvel. But the movement is not simple since, through the admiration of the self in his "work," he involuntarily becomes the admirer of his "work" itself. He becomes a lover not of Tourvel but of his own art represented in his "work," like an artist who contemplates his masterpiece. Thanks to its prolongation in time, the illusion is, in a sense, turned into truth, and identification within an aesthetic experience becomes the equivalent of empirical existence. As Valmont explains later on:

> Indeed, if first loves appear in general more virtuous and, as they say, more chaste; if they are at least slower in their progress; it is not, as people think, from delicacy or timidity, but because the heart, surprised by an unknown sentiment, hesitates as it were at every step to enjoy the charm it feels, and because this charm is so powerful upon a fresh heart that it forgets every other pleasure. This is so true, that a libertine in love—if a libertine can be in love—becomes at that very moment less eager to enjoy. In short there is only the difference of more and less between Danceny's conduct with the Volanges girl and mine with the chaste Madame de Tourvel. (2:57:106)

Love is first of all an aesthetic experience for young lovers as well as for the libertine Vicomte. Even though Valmont places more emphases on aesthetic effect, his role of libertine requires no less the quality of a good military man. For example, everything must be calculated and prepared as on a battlefield. But at the moment that the admiration of his own performance becomes a real passion, the self-discipline of a soldier disappears. Valmont can no longer remain the master either of "time" or of his partner, since he is mastered by passion, which induces him to destroy his fortress of the self. Through the identification with his "work," Mme. de Tourvel, Valmont identifies himself with a type of universal lover. In order to exculpate himself for falling in love with Tourvel he has to prove that any lover is not truly in love. There is no pure love, only a feeling of self-admiration. But, whatever the object of love, the effect remains the same: the spontaneous "charm" makes one forget the calculated "pleasure" of a successful project.

Price of Freedom: Slavery of the Self

We can see in the next chapter, the heroes of the Chinese erotic novel *The Golden Lotus,* Hsi-men Ch'ing and his kind are mainly interested in the gratification of their immediate desires. By contrast, the French libertines in *Les Liaisons dangereuses* can only experience a programmed and postponed pleasure, which requires self-control or even continence. In this sense, libertinism does not signify unlimited freedom, but rather a strong self-discipline.

Take as an example the "training program" of the Marquise de Merteuil in which she internalizes the restrictions of the social system and thus anticipates on a psychological level her own punishment by the same system. In other words, the very fortress of the self that protects her from the external world is also a psychological jail to which she confines herself.

However, the subjective world in which the libertines are all-powerful must be recognized by others in order to last.[20]

> The true libertinism, which is neither good fortunes nor sleeping-around, is the will to domination. Well, following the rules of the game, the domination can only be temporary: the death or the fall of the possessed object, the last "figure" of seduction, puts an end to it. That's why they need the lasting knowledge of an accomplice. This is the case of all the antisocial associations. The strength of the subjective world results from its invisibility—or impenetrability, which allows the subject to control others by his or her superior knowledge of them and by exploitation of their ignorance of themselves. This dilemma constitutes the weak point of the fortress of the self in the case of Laclos's libertines.

As we have seen, even though on a few occasions Merteuil may experience a certain emotion (such as jealousy), her relationships with the world are mainly based on a radical pragmatism, albeit a pragmatism which is practiced in a world of leisure and almost devoid of any economic concerns.

The only event that has a practical nature is her lawsuit against certain of her husband's junior relatives in regard to her inheritance. But this is not part of her game. The only justification of this feature of the plot is the ending: Merteuil's loss of property as a providential punishment to add to her physical deformation.

Merteuil's game, by its lack of any material concern, resembles a highly competitive sport: the winner is the one who knows most and most successfully keeps his or her own truth from others. To become the winner, Merteuil needs, first of all, to study her society carefully; she must set a double standard between "being" and "appearance," which corresponds to the double standard of social reality.

In addition to her exercises of self-control, her learning consists of two different parts—reading and life experience. The book learning must be tested by her own observations, which, in turn, must be further extended by reading. She writes to the Vicomte:

> I supported them with the assistance of reading; but do not think that it was all of the kind you suppose. I studied our manners in novels, our opinions in philosophers; I even sought in the severest moralists what it was they exacted of us and in this way I learned that one could do, what one ought to think and what one ought to appear. (2:81:163–64)

For the Marquise, everything, including the act of reading, is based primarily on a principle of utilitarianism. Valmont, however, must believe that main part of her reading list ought to consist of libertine literature since this may give her more pleasure. Nevertheless, she does not read for her own pleasure but mainly according to a principle of utilitarianism in order to "fortify" her observations in life.

For the Marquise books offer a way to understand various people, partly because books describe people, but also because many people let themselves be guided by books. For her, books, like people, are merely instruments to gain useful knowledge of the world. To this extent, libertine books are of little interest to her, because she does not need very often to resort to reading to understand the mind the libertine, which she already understands by the analogy of her own mind.

To read things which please her in this case is a mere waste, because this does not help her gain more knowledge or, more precisely, more power. She prefers to spend her time studying people situated further from her way of thinking and whose opinions may have a strong impact on society, such as "the severest moralists." Only by studying their restrictions can she learn how to break them.

The principle that guides the Marquise's life is the same as the one that guides her reading. In reducing others to instruments of her pleasure, she, first of all, transforms herself into an instrument by sacrificing pleasure to usefulness. Her only pleasure is the pleasure of power, inherently a pleasure of both master and slave. Based as it is on a strict mastery of the self, it involves the renunciation of self-indulgence.

Indeed, Merteuil learns much more from her life experiences than from the intellectual world of reading; as she says herself:

> I entered society, an unmarried girl, at a time when my condition compelled me to silence and inaction; I made use of it to observe and to reflect. While I was thought lightheaded or inattentive because I paid little attention to the conversations they were careful to hold with me, I carefully gathered those they tried to hide from me. (2:81:161)

Merteuil's career of libertinism starts with her careful observation of the world. Motivated mainly by a sense of rebellion against her condition as a woman who is "compelled to silence and inaction," she, at first, transforms the world into the object of her observation and reflection instead of allowing herself to become a passive object.

Later on, that world becomes the scene of her actions. She learns through her observations that "being" and "appearance" do not correspond in society, and one must adjust oneself to this fundamental divergence. There is no point to understanding truth, since truth is merely a commonly accepted lie.

Naturally, she is not at all interested in others' understanding of her true personality, but in their misunderstanding. To this extent, understanding people who differ from her is crucial in both her life and in her reading. Hence, as a young and beautiful libertine, Merteuil chooses to play the role of a prude and to observe the somewhat puritanical world of old women. In her letters to Valmont she repeatedly talks about them,[21] offering an analysis that appears to be not only perspicacious but also, to a certain degree, impartial.

When Valmont suspects his old aunt of acting against him, because he believes that age makes a woman harsh, Merteuil becomes a good defender of old ladies. By praising them she is not acknowledging the qualities of her enemies in terms of morality but rather the functions or the usefulness of her instruments.

Her principle is primarily utilitarian; she is not constrained by an inflexible ideology or moral standards. People are commodities which have only exchange values but no moral values. As a result, human feelings and emotions are also commodified. Even curiosity is useful in exchange for knowledge, another means by which she can gain power. She explains in her letter:

> That useful curiosity which served to instruct me, also taught me to dissimulate; I was often forced to conceal the objects of my attention from the eyes of those about me and I tried to direct my own eyes at will; from this I gained that ability to simulate when I chose that preoccupied gaze you have praised so often. Encouraged by this first success, I tried to govern the different expressions of my face in the same way. Did I experience some grief, I studied to show an air of serenity, even one of joy; I carried my zeal so far as to cause myself voluntary pain and to seek for an expression of pleasure at the same time. I worked over myself with the same care and more trouble to repress the symptoms of an unexpected joy. In this way I acquired that power over my features by which I have sometimes seen you astonished. (2:81:161)

The crucial element in her life is "will"—will to domination. She can dominate the objective world only by dominating her subjective world—more rigorously. Her masochistic gesture of "causing voluntary pain" reminds us of Julien Sorel who voluntarily imposes pain on himself to punish a moment of sincerity.[22]

These two characters share a common point of view; only one who is stronger than others may free oneself from the servitude of society, and one who wants to be stronger has to become more hypocritical. Thus, strict training in hypocrisy is the price of freedom.

If Julien fails, it is because he does not completely overcome his sincerity. If Merteuil fails, it is because she cannot completely overcome the desire to be understood and appreciated as a human being by at least one other human being: Valmont.

Julien wins more sympathy from his readers than Merteuil. Whereas Stendhal's hero fights for power and his own interests at a practical level, Laclos's heroine indulges in wickedness for its own sake. Furthermore, Merteuil seems to have perfected the art of hypocrisy, but Julien can hardly repress certain spontaneous feelings. In other words, the Marquise is more hateful largely because she is more successful, especially as a female intruder in the world of power-game traditionally reserved for the opposite sex.

As we have seen, the masochistic gesture in the case of the Marquise is preventive, whereas Julien's is punitive. It goes without saying that Merteuil's satanic perfection in searching for evil appears much more uncanny than Julien's desire for social power, which is further humanized by his failure. However, in both cases, the individual is doomed to alienation.

If one makes oneself conform to social rules, one becomes the slave of social conditions. An individual rebelling against society must first imitate the very shortcoming of society—hypocrisy—to get on an equal footing with his or her rival. Moreover, it is the society that pushes both Sorel and Merteuil to choose this individual form of rebellion. Neither can exploit a collective action—because of the failure of the Revolution in the case of Julien, and because of her condition as a woman in the case of the Marquise.

If Valmont is less extreme than his female accomplice in this aspect, his pleasure is no less programmed. As on a battlefield, strategy is best calculated beforehand, Valmont tries to prevent surprise.

> I left nothing to chance except from consideration of a great advantage in case of success and from the certainty of other resources in case of defeat. (4:125:279)

It seems to Valmont that there is no true pleasure except in victories—victories achieved at the cost of spontaneous enjoyments and self-gratification, for these contradict the libertine principle of self-control. For example, in spite of his attachment to Tourvel and the happiness that a spontaneous relationship brings him, Valmont does not hesitate a moment to copy the letter dictated by Merteuil to break off with her. In this case, his vanity—or his image of the constructed world of a libertine self—is more important that his more primitive needs. The two—the gratification of desire and his image of self—are incompatible. As the Marquise writes:

> I admit freely that this triumph flatters me more than all those I have obtained up till now. You will perhaps think I value this woman very highly after having formerly rated her so low: not at all; I have not obtained this advantage over her, but over you; that is the amusing thing and it is really delicious. (4:145:316–17)

On the one hand, the Marquise is right in proclaiming her victory over the Vicomte, since Tourvel *is* Valmont's mirror-image as his best "actress" and his "work." Valmont is unique only through Tourvel's "acting" directed by her careful seducer. By destroying his unique "work," she reduces the "author" into a kind of banality.

On the other hand, the Marquise does not necessarily triumph over the Vicomte. Rather, his desire to project a cosmic image of himself triumphs over a desire that is rooted at a deeper and more spontaneous level. To a large extent, Valmont's victory in his libertine game always requires the same kind of sacrifice of spontaneous pleasure, but usually on a smaller scale. Libertinism, in this case, is a special kind of continence:

> I therefore maintained a calm which would have done honor to the continence of Scipio. (1:44:83)

Like Scipio, the Vicomte sacrifices his pleasure to a cause. This gesture requires the same kind of devotion and the same kind of discipline. The only difference is that Scipio sacrifices desire for the sake of morality, whereas Valmont does the same thing in order to profane moral values more efficiently.

For Merteuil, as well as for Valmont, the self-sufficient subjective world is only a myth. A human being, however confident he or she may be, always has to resort to external recognition to valorize himself or herself.[23] On the other hand a human being commands worship only to the extent that he or she is wrapped in a certain mystery. As recognition is contrary to mystery, demystification is inevitable.

However much Valmont admires the Marquise, his admiration is based on his knowledge of her capacity, not on faith. Whereas faith requires an infinity of distance, the act of knowing reduces the distance between subject and object. Indeed, by its very nature, understanding something entails a critical act. At the same time, without Valmont's recognition, Merteuil's power remains meaningless. Since "meaning" necessarily implies communication, an uncommunicable meaning can only exist in madness. In short, his knowledge is both the basis of the existence of her supreme power and the potential force of its destruction.

Given their relationship, one asks a difficult but also trivial question: is the Marquise in love with the Vicomte?

She is in love, not with Valmont himself, but rather with her own image as reflected in the eyes of her partner, since the latter is the only person in this world who is able to appreciate her as she is in reality.

Because of her jealousy, some critics discover in her heart the existence of passion.[24] But jealousy does not necessarily keep pace with passion, especially in the case of the Marquise, whose passionate self-idolatry probably overshadows all her other feelings.

For example, Belleroche is, for her, no more important than a masculine *"machine à plaisir."* It would be very hard to say that Merteuil is in love with him, but she is no less jealous. Simply because Belleroche finds the Vicomtess "pretty," the Marquise wants to punish her potential rival by a scandal:

> Moreover, I have reason to complain of her. The Chevalier de Belleroche thinks her prettier than I like. (2:74:138)

This disproportion between the "cause" and "effect" results, to a large extent, from the disproportion between the importance that she attaches to her subjective world and the importance that she attaches to other people. She is the center.

Except for Valmont, the chosen witness of her power, others exist merely as instruments or as objects of revenge.

At the same time, one may also say that Merteuil is in love with Valmont, because love, indeed, often has a narcissistic undertone. She loves Valmont as someone loves a handy and indispensable instrument, or a unique object of a special pleasure.

Valmont's understanding of Merteuil's art of deceiving increases his admiration for her technique while decreasing his awe for her person. For example, her art of dissimulation is useless in the scene where Valmont discovers her flirting with Danceny in "the little house". (4:151:330)

Even her position in the avenging act is considerably weakened by her eagerness to obtain the admiration of the "connoisseur" of her power. In this sense, Valmont becomes a "masculine Delilah" who takes the hair of a "female Samson" in his hand. Because of their dependence on the look or recognition of the other, the libertines find that look all the more threatening.

As a result, Merteuil's tremendous efforts are turned into a sterile intellectual game, cruel for herself as well as for her victims. Laclos's heroine desires a godlike position within human society, but, being human herself, she ultimately fails to bear a godlike loneliness. Had she succeeded, however, we would not have had the chance to read Laclos's novel—at least not in its epistolary form.

2

Dispersal of Desire:
Dissemination of the Self

L*es Liaisons dangereuses*[1] and *The Golden Lotus*[2] share a similar point: both describe perverse sexual relationships in a more or less clinical way. Eroticism itself is a form of violation of social norms, which is largely determined by its object of violation. As a result, this similar point of departure makes the differences between the French and the Chinese novels only more striking, taking into account the differences in their cultural and ethical backgrounds.

The libertines in *Les Liaisons dangereuses* seem to live in a world practically free of financial concern. Since what they transgress is the "spirituality" of love, the transgression itself appears "purged" of material concerns. At the same time, this transgression consists of turning human feelings into commodities by treating them as instruments which they use in their libertine game. Nevertheless, this reification is realized at a highly conceptual level.

Conversely, the erotic relationships between the hero and his numerous lovers in *The Golden Lotus* materialize desire in the form of a monetary system. The hero of the *Chin P'ing Mei* is named Hsi-men Ch'ing. A rich merchant, he lives with his six wives and innumerable lovers in his large household and also has some connections with powerful figures. Since Hsi-men Ch'ing's object of transgression—the Confucian ethics of moderation—is more concerned with the practical aspects of human wisdom and moral rules resolving problems in everyday life, the excessive quality of Hsi-men's desire is best symbolized in terms of currency. The Chinese hero not only buys his sexual partners (including his wives) but also expresses his unique tenderness toward his favorite wife, Li P'ing-erh, through money. In fact, Hsi-men is a diligent merchant—not of any other goods, but of sex. By turning his household into a sex market, he transgresses the structure of traditional family, which is the basis of Chinese society.

In the world of the novel, almost everyone appears to accept the principle of material gain and loss in sexual relations. In the case of prostitutes, this is acknowledged explicitly; in the case of the adulterous wives of Hsi-men's servants or his own wives—some of whom are former prostitutes—it is acknowledged implicitly.

The market principle not only determines Hsi-men's sexual relations but also justifies his excessive desire. Just as he buys women with coinage, he also buys moral support for his immoral behavior from the so-called "supernatural world." In fact, the transcendental world of Buddhism and Taoism in the novel is contaminated by the corrupted value of coin. Wealth becomes the icon of the spiritual prosperity in a Buddhist temple, and spirituality, like human affection, has to be expressed in coinage.

Power, rather than money, plays the dominant role in *Les Liaisons dangereuses*. What is at stake in the French novel is primarily psychological domination. The psychological power wielded by Merteuil and Valmont can be considered as the counter-model of the preromantic self in Rousseau's novel and is traceable all the way back to the Christian notion of consciousness.

By contrast, Hsi-men Ch'ing's strength in sexual relations is materialized by money and social position. Hsi-men's perverse power transgresses the Confucian ethics of family values and moral integrity. This power—which cannot be dissociated from money—expresses itself through the violence done to the flesh of his sexual partners.

As in the case of the French libertines in Laclos's novel, the notion of pleasure is always associated with power. But what is at stake in the Chinese novel is not the pleasure of wielding a psychological power over partners, but the privilege of indulging in gratification, in most cases to the detriment of the weaker party.

While Valmont and Merteuil desire to be "loved" or "worshiped" by their partners, Hsi-men requires from his lovers the verbal recognition of his absolute authority. The French libertines hope that the affection of their victims toward them is "unique," "genuine," and "original"—even though their own feelings, as the product of performance, are characterized by artificiality. Hsi-men, by contrast, contents himself with the apparent respect for his absolute authority on the part of his lovers, be it obtained through financial or political power.

Whereas the French libertines' desire for control over others can be fulfilled only through self-control, Hsi-men Ch'ing's desire is characterized by its immediate and dispersed nature. The overwhelming importance of the material aspect of desire very often makes the hero unable to name his desire, except through its concrete object. But as soon as the hero takes possession of the object in question, it loses its symbolic dimension; he must ceaselessly seek new objects in order to overcome a feeling of void.

The objects in his possession become indistinguishable from one another. Lacking any distinctive qualitative or psychological characteristics, the women he sleeps with are reduced to a similar object of the flesh; and his endless conquests become a hopeless gesture of repetition. In the Confucian tradition, names, as the incarnation of social law and authority, must be respected. For example, the name "father" implies a series of rules that determine the behavior of the individual bearing this name. Moreover, social authorities, such as a prince, are considered the only people having the right to decide the relationship between a word and its meaning. Thus, the act of "naming" is theoretically almost constitutionalized. But Hsi-men uses his name of "adopted father" to facilitate his sexual relations and his name of "adopted son" to acquire social power. In this case, the act of naming and the name itself are violated at different levels. Hsi-men's violation of the act of naming, leads to a "dissemination" of the self, a dissolution of the family, and, obliquely, the disintegration of the country.

Marketable Eros

Money, in *The Golden Lotus*, does not simply mean "coin," "silver" or "gold," although the materiality of money itself is overwhelmingly important. In exchange for currency, Hsi-men Ch'ing very often receives the sexual favors of women (and eventually of men) of various ranks, sometimes including his own wives and especially his fifth wife, P'an Chin-lien.

Conversely, sexuality sometimes becomes the means by which Hsi-men acquires money. But at the same time, eroticism is reinforced—even embellished by money, as in his relationship with his sixth wife, Li P'ing-erh. In other words, currency is not only the representation of material wealth but also of physical pleasure; it equates Hsi-men's unlimited desire with the open-endedness and abstraction of numbers. Indeed, the spiritual value, either moral or religious, is envisioned here as equal to an infinite amount of gold.

Take, as an example, the case of repairing the Yung-fu Temple, considered in the book as the icon of the Buddhist Paradise. The prosperity of the temple is paradoxically measured by material abundance rather than by any transcendent value. Moreover, this exchange is based on a system, called "retribution (*pao*)[a]." "Retribution" can be applied both to the act of repaying a benevolent deed or the act of taking revenge. The one who does a good deed will be rewarded, and the one who does a bad deed will be punished, either in this life or the next, in proportion to the degree of goodness or evil. In terms of "retribution" (*pao*), all human actions, including virtues, are a medium of exchange. The world itself is even reduced to an immense monetary system in which every element is not only interchangeable with currency, but also functions as currency.

For Hsi-men Ch'ing, there is no qualitative difference between the possession of gold or silver and that of a woman. Both the metal and the flesh are tangible and concrete. Similarly, it is difficult for him to distinguish gustatory pleasure from sexual enjoyment: both are momentary and physical. The difference between a human body and a rare metal or a delicious dish is not of substance but only of degree, in that sexual pleasure is more intense for the hero than the enjoyment of any other material things.

An example can be provided by Hsi-men's relationship with P'an Chin-lien, his fifth wife, a woman of exceptional sexual appeal and one who knows how to use that appeal to manipulate Hsi-men.

The novel opens by presenting Chin-lien's background and immediately follows with the scene of her flirtation with Hsi-men. That she is from a poor and lower class family—her mother is the widow of a tailor—makes her situation more crudely similar to that of an article in a market. When he sees the beautiful wife of the dwarf merchant, Hsi-men expresses his admiration in the following terms:

What a female! How can I get my hands on her? (1:2:53)

The term "get my hands on" (*tao shou*)[b] refers to concrete objects of possession. To make love with a desirable woman is to possess her body in the most materialist sense of the word. Moreover, the term used here for "female" (*tz'u-erh*)[c] suggests an animal-like quality. In other words, the relationship between Hsi-men and his object of desire is completely commercialized, and, in fact, dehumanized.

Acquiring Chin-lien is a question of how much silver one needs to spend, and whether or not the article is worth such a price. As long as Hsi-men finds her valuable, he is willing to pay; and if he is willing to pay, he can have his "female." The flirtation is thus reduced to a market exchange, in which the woman's moral or personal motivation does not figure.

Hsi-men's first step in the seduction is to "buy" with silver Chin-lien's neighbor, Wang P'o, so the old woman can serve as a go-between.

"Even if I have to part with several *liang*[3] of silver to thank her, it won't be too great a price." (1:2:53)

Hsi-men's powerful attraction to Chin-lien's sensual beauty—he has come back more than ten times since he first saw her—is not allowed to get in the way of good business: expenses must be accurately calculated. Moreover, Hsi-men is not the only one who follows the logic of the sex market so crudely. The old woman, wise to Hsi-men's longing for her beautiful neighbor, immediately starts to contemplate how much money she can extract from the lewd and rich merchant. Furthermore, P'an Chin-lien herself not only has no objection to being treated as a commodity, but she relishes her ability to exchange her "product" for financial benefit.

This relationship continues even after her marriage. When she pleases her husband during a sexual bout, she always asks for money to buy cloth which enhances her beauty. (2:40:53, 3:52:301, 4:74:484).

In this sense, the money the master spends on her benefits him—or at least embellishes his precious object. It is thus "worthwhile" (*chih-te*)[d]—a good investment. Still thanks to her art of manipulation, Chin-lien partially reverses this active-passive relationship by the end of the book. From a passive object of desire, she sometimes becomes Hsi-men's master of desire.

In many cases, the relationship between the buyer and the seller of sexual favors may be much cruder, as in Hsi-men Ch'ing's relationship with Sung Hui-lien, who is his maid and the wife of his servant.

The woman lifted the door curtain and went into Yüeh-niang's room. She saw Hsi-men Ch'ing sitting on a chair, drinking. She moved forward and sat in his legs brusquely. They kissed each other and embraced. The woman held his privates and at the same time plied him with wine from her own mouth. She said, "Father,[4] if you still have fragrant tea, please give me some more. What you have given me the day before yesterday is used up." Then, she continued, "I owe several *ch'ien*[5] of silver to sister Hsüeh for some flowers. If you have any money, please give me some so that I will be able to pay her back." Hsi-men answered, "In my bag I still have one or two *liangs* left; you can take them." At the same time, he tried to take off her trousers. (2:23:58)

The scene is rich in parallel actions. On the one hand, Hui-lien excites Hsi-men with her hand and at the same time asks for money with her mouth, which alternately kisses and begs. On the other hand, Hsi-men makes promises with his mouth and tries to accelerate the action with his hands.

Both "at the same time" (*yi-mien*)[e] and "in saying" (*Shuo-che*)[f] emphasize the simultaneity of actions. In this situation, sex is no longer so much a taboo object of conversation, although the characters certainly have no interest in a scientific discussion of sexuality: they are mainly interested in discussing its price.

This kind of sexual relationship is usually associated with prostitution, but for prostitutes, the market is institutionalized according to a well-accepted logic—albeit one that excludes their products from "decent" society. For the maids in Hsi-men's household, by contrast, there are no specified commercial rules, and prostitution becomes the norm of the household.

This fact may explain why all the singing girls who visit Hsi-men's home are not treated too differently from his wives. Some of his wives are themselves former prostitutes. In the logic of that house, prostitutes are like everyone else. Market principles prevail, and there is no line of demarcation between a "decent" woman and an "indecent" one. The predominance of money, then, abolishes any sense of decorum.

On the whole, Hui-lien's art of selling her own body—her business acumen—remains primitive. She does not know how to calculate advantage and disadvantage in order to extract the maximum from the master. Although she is not stupid, she is often too preoccupied with some immediate interest, such as how to satisfy her childish vanity by wresting the most from the situation.

If Hsi-men and his kind in the Chinese novel are not so interested in postponing sexual gratification to achieve a psychological conquest as are Laclos's libertines, at least some of their sexual partners are willing to postpone satisfaction of their material cravings in order to manipulate them more efficiently to achieve those financial aims.

Wang Liu-erh, the middle aged wife of Hsi-men's servant is much more skillful at this than the inexperienced Hui-lien. In fact, she is inexperienced only in comparison with other persons in the novel. Liu-erh consciously ''sells'' her body to Hsi-men, calculating how to derive as much material advantage as possible from each pleasure that she gives him. One day, Hsi-men visits her in her house, and they have a chat before sexual intercourse.

> Hsi-men said, ''Recently, I saw the wine that you bought here is not too drinkable. So I asked them to send this pot of wine.'' The woman made a curtsy and said, ''Thank you very much for the wine. You are absolutely right. We are useless persons and only capable of living in this out-of-the-way place. There is no good shop here, how can one get some proper wine? We can only buy wine from other large streets.'' Hsi-men said, ''When your husband comes back, you can discuss it with him. Tell him I will spend some money to help you buy a house on Shih-tzu street. So both of you can move there. The store where he works will be close, and it will also be very easy to do shopping. Everything will be more convenient.'' The woman said, ''Well, you are right, father. If we can leave here thanks to your pity, we will be better off. Even for you, father, you can come without worrying about the gossips of villains.'' (2:38:458)

Unlike Hui-lien, the cunning woman here seems to lead Hsi-men by the nose. She knows his weakness for the combination of good wine, delicious food, and beautiful women. No doubt, his favorite wife, Li P'ing-erh's, habit of taking expensive wine and food while having sexual intercourse contributes to her irresistible attractiveness in Hsi-men's eyes.

By emphasizing her husband's inability to buy a house near a good liquor store, Liu-erh exploits his own selfish motivations to get him to spend more money on her. She kills two birds with one stone. First, the servant flatters the master's vanity. As the one who is capable of buying a house for them, he is the opposite of ''useless,'' the word she uses to describe her husband. Second, she desires a new house for its location near a good wine shop, that is not for herself but for the comfort and gratification of the master.

Liu-erh, in other words, has convinced her customer to believe—paradoxically—that the more he spends, the more he gains. By enticing Hsi-men to spend more money on her, she elevates her own price as a sex object in his eyes.

Later on, Liu-erh convinces her husband to take advantage of Hsi-men's death to embezzle a large amount of money.

> From the ancient time on, if there were such a thing called "the principle of heaven," we would have nothing to eat. Moreover, he had my body in his possession for a long time. There is nothing wrong with using some of his money. (5:81:9)

Put otherwise, sentiment has no place where business is concerned. Understanding this, Liu-erh is one of the very few people in the book who ends her life peacefully. By opposing "the principle of heaven" which, in this context, means the minimum ethical criterion, to the needs of everyday life, such as "eating," she reveals deep insight into the principle that governs the world of the novel. If you want to "eat"—a metaphor for living a comfortable life—you must ignore all moral rules.

Indeed, in *The Golden Lotus*, the one or two characters who safeguard a moral sense are seriously punished. The censor Ts'eng—the only one who ever wanted to punish Hsi-men and his kind for their outrageous crimes—is himself vilified as criminal and sent to a remote place to die in jail: "having nothing to eat," to use Liu-erh's expression.

Moreover, Liu-erh's lack of sentimentality toward a recently dead lover is perfectly justifiable in accordance with the dominant logic in Hsi-men's household. Who has ever seen a "piece of merchandise" express condolence for its owner? In this system of exchange, human attachment is merely a luxury.

In this respect, Hsi-men's world is completely different from Valmont's and Merteuil's world of the libertine game. The world of *Les Liaisons dangereuses* is free, so to speak, of any financial concerns, whereas the dominant principle in *The Golden Lotus* is nothing else but money. However, the two novels share a similarity: the perverse nature of the game. The difference is that the French libertines play with a psychological power, whereas the Chinese master plays with a financial one.

Despite the intricate relationship between money and sex, Hsi-men does once experience some genuine tenderness that is apparently free of direct financial concerns. This is in the case of his sixth wife, Li P'ing-erh. In this relationship, unlike all the others, the woman is the one who pays but not the one who gets paid: she has the greater personal wealth of the two.

Although Hsi-men's exaggerated mourning for P'ing-erh exasperates almost all his other wives, he is nevertheless incapable of analyzing his own feelings about her. He associates her with various good things—such as a lost son and gradually disappearing prosperity. Moreover, a sentimental song is more expressive of his feelings toward P'ing-erh than his own language, and theatrical performance moves him to shed tears for her.

Once, after a song, his fair-weather friend, Ying Po-chüeh, notices his sadness and inquires about the cause. Hsi-men's answer is revealing.

> You only blame me when I talk about her. If she had been alive, she would have prepared my dishes herself. After her death, they leave servants alone to manage this. You see what this looks like. Not a single piece is really tasty. (4:65:179)

He lacks the language to give direct voice to his feelings of tenderness for his dead wife, and thus, he must project his emotions onto a concrete object in one way or another. His sorrow for P'ing-erh becomes, therefore, his nostalgia for good dishes or for money.

Tai-an, his closest servant and who knows his most secret thoughts, explains to salesman Fu, the manager of Hsi-men's drugstore:

> Why does our master feel so sorrowful? Not because of the dead person but because of her money. (4:64:130)

Certainly, this statement has some truth to it. P'ing-erh's money had, in a certain sense, bought her equality with Hsi-men. Without this minimum of equality, Hsi-men would not have developed his relatively strong attachment to her and would probably have treated her as an object of use only to satisfy his desire. Usually, once the utilitarian function disappears, the object is forgotten. P'ing-erh would have been forgotten as were so many other lovers, because, in this regard, Hsi-men's memory is not notoriously good.

On the surface, this case seems to present the exception to Hsi-men's exchange system. In reality, P'ing-erh's situation can be considered a reversed version of the market principles operating in Hsi-men's household.

On the one hand, P'ing-erh, despite her money, can buy her satisfaction only from Hsi-men. "You are the balm of my life," she repeatedly says, characterizing their relationship. As in the case of a serious sickness that can be cured only by a single medicine, Hsi-men is the only one who can satisfy her otherwise insatiable sexual hunger.

On the other hand, P'ing-erh is irreplaceable for Hsi-men because she is an exception who combines both objects of his most intense desire—extreme wealth and great beauty.

After her death, Hsi-men's best way of expressing his sadness is to arrange an expensive funeral. The money spent on ritual substantializes his feelings and summarizes the "this-world" relationship between him and his favorite woman; not only sex, but any relationships can be reduced to a monetary equivalent. The same logic allows us to better understand Hsi-men's delight when he sees people admiring the magnificence of his favorite wife's funeral.

The multiple functions of money in the sexual relationships of the hero extend to other areas as well, including the spiritual. He finds support for his idolatry of money even in a Buddhist prayer text written by Chuo-hsi, the monk of the highest rank in the Yung-fu Temple, for the occasion of soliciting donations to repair the temple.

The Buddha worshiped in the Yung-fu Temple (or Temple of Everlasting Happiness) is called "Wan-hui" ("coming back from ten thousand *li*").[6] When Wan-hui was a little boy, his old mother became sick because she missed her elder son, a soldier living on the border. In order to calm the misgivings of his mother, Wan-hui went to the border and brought a letter from his old brother after a journey of several thousand kilometers accomplished within a single day. This ethical deed wins him both the name of "Wan-hui" and the Buddhahood.

One can say that he "bought" his Buddhahood with a good deed, in accordance with the central value of Confucian morality: filial piety. In this sense, the worship in this temple is initially based on an exchange between an ethical value in this world (Confucian morality) and a religious value rooted in otherworldliness (Buddhahood).

Chuo-hsi, the one who writes the Buddhist text here, is described in the novel as a "venerable saintly monk from the Paradise of the West" (*hsi-tien lao sheng-seng*).[g] (3:57:461) He has come from India, which, as the source of Buddhism, is usually considered in China as identifiable with the Paradise of the West. It takes him eight or nine years to walk from his own country to China, for which he has an "admiration" (*mou*).[h] (3:57:459)

Ironically, what the "saint monk" admires in China is not "purity" (*ch'ing*)[i]—as the author says in the novel—but the debased world of Hsi-men's household corrupted by money. The itinerary of the Indian monk in *The Golden Lotus* is similar to that of the saintly monk of the T'ang, the Master Tripitaka in the *Hsi-yu chi*,[7] but in a reverse direction.

These two novels share another element in common: the iconic function of money in the Buddhist world. In the *Hsi-yu chi*, after a long journey and innumerable adversities, the *sutras* the pilgrims receive are without any characters: the pilgrims have failed to bribe the *arhats* in charge of keeping *sutras* in paradise. Moreover, the Buddhist world is very often represented in the *Hsi-yu chi* in terms of its material magnificence. In both cases, the spiritual value of paradise is mainly a function of its greater wealth in comparison with the earth.

Ironically, after the "venerable saintly monk" has spent eight years on his trip toward China, nine years in speechless meditation—altogether seventeen years, the same number of years as the Tripitaka's pilgrimage—his first "idea" (*nien-t'ou*)[j] (3:57:465) consists of begging money from Hsi-men to reconstruct the temple.

Usually, Hsi-men shows little faith in Buddhism and prefers to ridicule this religion through its representatives, the nuns who have close relationships with his wives. This attitude apparently changes for a short period after the birth of his only son, Kuan-ke. The boy's health is fragile, and he does everything to protect it. Chuo-hsi takes advantage of this occasion to convince the hero through a promise of worldly happiness.

> I remember it is said in Buddhist *sutra*, if the believers, men or women in this world, enjoy charity by giving money to restore Buddha's statues, they are entitled to have noble offspring. (3:57:465)

Thus, Chuo-hsi begins his career in China as a salesman. The only difference between him and a real salesman is that he promotes intangible hope instead of tangible goods.

Anyone, believer or not, can be his customer. He is ready to sell the hope of worldly happiness as well as that of access to the Paradise of the West to a thief or a murderer. So long as he or she is willing to pay, he or she becomes "good" (*shan*)[k] in Buddhist terms.

Unfortunately for Hsi-men, the intangible hope that he has purchased with silver does not materialize: his son dies within one year. While Chuo-hsi refers to Buddhist *sutra* to justify his false promise, Hsi-men finds in the discourse of the "saintly monk" some support for his own value system. For, if there is no connection between the monk's promise and the result, there is a perfect connection between the Buddhist discourse and Hsi-men's own declaration. In other words, the hero cannot buy the life of his son from the other world, but at least he can buy moral support from the allegedly "supernatural world" for his immoral behavior.

Let us now compare Chuo-hsi's following statement seeking donation with Hsi-men's later speech of self-justification:

> Here is the Yung-fu Temple, the terrain where Buddhas in ancient time preached, holy place of spiritual cultivation. Constructed by the Liang Wu Emperor, inaugurated by the Buddhist master Wan-hui, the temple was impressively magnificent. The ground of the Jetavana Garden was covered with gold with refined engravings. It looked like the original garden in the Buddhist world. Around the mansion, stairs were made in jade. The buildings were so high that they reached up to the ninth heaven. Clouds surrounded the temple, and the palace of Ta-hsiung might con-

tain thousands of monks. The annexed houses were magnificent. There were everywhere edifices with indigo blue roofs. The corridors were very clean. In fact, it was more refined than an earthly paradise. At that time bells rang and drums resounded. All agreed: "It is the Buddhist kingdom in the human world." (3:57:466)

According to Chuo-hsi, Buddha's prestige is complemented by the name of a human authority, an emperor. Moreover, the rise and fall of Buddhism in this temple is marked by the material abundance of the past and by its present impoverishment. Wealth is so highly esteemed that spirituality itself is measured by the criterion of gain and loss.

As a result, a symbol of Buddhist worship, the temple, is transformed into an icon of the Buddhist paradise, since "it looks like the Original Garden in the Buddhist world" in its worldly splendor. Thus the relationship between the signified and signifier is analogical, manifested in material riches, as in "ground covered with gold."

Even the contact between the human world of earth and the spiritual world of heaven is made through the impressive height of the temple, which indicates more material riches than spiritual elevation. In this sense, the Paradise of the West incarnated by its earthly image, the Yung-fu Temple, is tantamount to infinite wealth; and the worship of gold tends to eclipse the worship of Buddhas in the context of this novel.

Viewed in this context, Chuo-hsi's statement dovetails with Hsi-men's "philosophy of life," and it is not surprising that Hsi-men is extremely pleased by the monk's speech. Immediately after his reading of Chuo-hsi's prayer, Hsi-men uses the monk's argument to answer the objection of his official wife, Yüeh-niang, to his immoral behavior.

Don't you know that even heaven and earth are also composed of *yin* and *yang*?[8] It is natural that man and woman get together. In this life, flirting and adultery are due mostly to a fate determined in former lives, listed in the book of marriage. Naturally, this is not because people willy-nilly force these kinds of relationships following their whim. I have heard that the difference of the Buddhas' Paradise of the West is only marked by its ground covered with gold. In the ten counts of hell, judges ask also for paper money. So long as I take advantage of our property to do extensively good deeds, I remain very rich, even if I raped the Divinity of Moon and the Weaving Lady in heaven and seduced the daughter of the Goddess of the West. (3:57:472)

Hsi-men repeats Chuo-hsi's expression "ground covered by gold." Instead of referring to the monk by name, he transforms this into a form of hearsay: "I have heard" (*tsan wen na*).[1] For Hsi-men, it makes no difference whether it is question of hearsay or a Buddhist saying, so long as it supports his value system.

Speech itself becomes another form of currency because, like coinage, it is anonymous and amoral. Chuo-hsi's argument—which in his opinion supports the value system of the Buddhist Paradise—becomes the justification of Hsi-men's immoral behavior. The payment that Hsi-men has made for the reparation of the Yung-fu Temple legitimizes his appropriation of the Buddhist discourse, which now circulates as a form of credit—and credibility—-in the world of the novel.

Later, he returns to the Buddhist universe of the monk's statement: he fancies raping all the divine beauties, be they Buddhist, Taoist, or simply mythological. In other words, if the quintessence of paradise is measured in terms of money, it can also be materialized in the imagination of the hero as the desirability of sensual beauty.

Indeed, Hsi-men's linkage with the Buddhist world is concerned mainly with sex. In chapter 49, another mysterious Indian monk of inescapably phallic appearance, uses a magic potion to provide Hsi-men with seemingly unlimited sexual energy.[9] In a sense, the phallic monk is a mystified image of the hero, since the latter will be eulogized as a personified penis by his "fair-weather" friends. (4:84:793)

In short, if paradise for the monk signifies unlimited abundance, Hsi-men simply adds one more item to the picture: satisfaction of all desire. Both of them assume that the ends can be reached exclusively by money. Since wealth represents paradise or the "supreme good," every crime becomes permitted. If one can buy access to paradise with coinage, why not also exchange women with the same medium?

This notion of "exchange" is comparable to the idea of "Retribution" (*pao*), which Martinson described as a "moral grammar."[10] The only difference is that, in Hsi-men's world, the exchange functions by means of currency, whereas the concept of *pao* is supposedly both ethical and religious. Indeed, everything is exchangeable in terms of *pao*, which might, in fact, also be translated by the English word "pay."

For example, the monk, P'u-ching, is no doubt the least suspicious of the three major Buddhist figures in the novel—P'u-ching, Chuo-hsi, and the phallic Indian monk. But fifteen years after saving Wu Yüeh-niang, the widow of Hsi-men Ch'ing, from being raped by an evil creature, P'u-ching requires her to repay it by forfeiting her only son. In the system of *pao*, good deeds or bad deeds, including human beings, are reduced to a medium of exchange. In this sense, the metaphorical usage of "grammar" in Martinson's dissertation appears somewhat questionable in that *pao* in the novel can hardly be taken as a syntactical force.

Returning now to the Buddha Wan-hui, if Wan-hui succeeded in becoming a Buddha, he also "bought" this position with the ethically—thus worldly—good deed of showing filial piety to his old mother. But this good deed is not enough to maintain his temple and his believers. Both the temple and the disciples need the corrupt coin of Hsi-men to survive.

The position of the moral code in the world remains utterly abstract unless it can be embodied through a signifier which, in most cases, is money. The integrity—Wan-hui's sainthood, for example—is manifested in the riches of his temple. The other half of this equation, however, is that money, being corrupt, contaminates and even transforms the moral code as well as the ideal of Buddhahood. In other words, the monetary system is not formed in accordance with the model of *pao*, but rather the notion of *pao* is "derived" from the market model and, therefore, transforms ethics into exchange value.

If there is any metaphorical grammar in the book, it is more an economic one than a moral one, given that the exchange economy seems to govern every aspect of the world—family life, sexual relationships, political activity, morality, and also the supernatural world of Buddhism. *Pao,* as a hybrid system composed of moral, natural, and supernatural elements, is based on the same model of market exchange. At the same time, the market principle is highly decentralized, since there is no recognizable authoritative figure—only the abstract and anonymous value of money. The "grammar" of market economy, as a model of decentralization, leads the world more toward a disintegration than toward a synthesis.

Sexual Pleasure and Social Position

The notion of power is just as complicated and ambiguous in this novel as that of money, if only because of its complex relationship with money. One cannot single out power as an external force or explain it independently of money or pleasure. Power resides in all kinds of social relations, since it is the very product and manifestation of these relations.[11]

Hsi-men's social position is based on his "property," or economic power, which he uses as a kind of currency to reward his partners. Sexual potency, associated with violence, is one of his major weapons for maintaining his mastery over his partners; but his potency also results from his social position—in his relationships with singing girls, for example.

The mightiest one in a given situation—whether Hsi-men or his superiors—has the right to fulfill his desire, capricious or not, and, in most cases, to the detriment of the weaker party. What he seeks in these relationships is not so much of a powerful position or substance as a powerful image or name, expressed by the verbal recognition of his partners in respect to his authority.

Paradoxically, this power of "name" can be acquired only through "substance." Unlike Laclos's libertines who play the role of the tender lover to conquer the hearts of their victims, Hsi-men has no pretension to psychological power. He is only interested in the most concrete form of domination of his partners, whether by physical or political force.

For example, Li Kuei-chieh, an attractive singing girl, is a prostitute just starting her career. Hsi-men is her first customer, and he tries to please her by all means at the beginning. His method of conquest seems a little peculiar. Instead of claiming to be tender, he tries to impress the singing girl by his violent nature:

> You still haven't learned my skill. Except for my first wife, all the other wives and maids in my house, any time I want to beat them, I surely give them a good lesson. Twenty or thirty successive blows of the horsewhip is nothing. Occasionally, I even cut off their hair. (1:12:276)

Here, (*shou-tuan*)[m] may be translated as "skill" as well as "sexual prowess." This term refers to the means by which Hsi-men obtains obedience from his wives and servants. Violence is for him a quality of masculinity—and thus a means of seduction—because, to do violence to his partners, marks his possession of their body. In other words, he is legitimate owner of their flesh, thanks to his position as their husband and master.

At the same time, sexual potency is also a means which Hsi-men occasionally uses to do violence to his partners. In chapter 27, Hsi-men extracts obedience from Chin-lien precisely because he plays with her sexual frustration and shame. In a rather violent manner, Hsi-men excites her desire and refuses to satisfy her until she agrees to obey his will. In other words, the capacity to give or withdraw pleasure from a partner is also a form of power.

Sex, then, is not only the *instrument* of but one of the *forms* of power. As a victim of her own "violent" desire, Chin-lien is vulnerable to Hsi-men's sexual potency.

In *Les Liaisons dangereuses*, Tourvel's love for Valmont is "violent" in that it leads to her own death. But in the French novel, the interchangeability of desire and violence is based on a psychological power, whereas in *The Golden Lotus*, Chin-lien's frustration is mostly physical.

The gesture of cutting hair, mentioned in Hsi-men's boastful statement to the singing girl, implies both physical and symbolic power. Since in the Confucian tradition "body, hair, and skin are gifts from our parents," this act violates the authority of the parents. Because filial piety is the central value in Confucian society, this also means that Hsi-men assumes a higher authority than anyone else in the life of the one whose hair has been cut.

In some cases, power as the substitute for money may have only a negative usage as a forfeiture for the transgression of his law. For example, Chiang Chu-shan has married Hsi-men's favorite wife-to-be, Li P'ing-erh, who had lost the hope that Hsi-men would make good on his own promise of marriage. The doctor is punished by a payment exacted by Hsi-men in the name of justice (naturally, with forged evidence). Afterward, Hsi-men repeats to P'ing-erh several times:

> If you had married another person, I would not have been so angry. But why marry such a wretched dwarf? What are his capacities? (1:18:414)

In other words, what frustrates him most is not that he has lost P'ing-erh but rather that she chose someone else. His battle is over only when he obtains her verbal recognition of his superiority. He asked:

> "I ask you who is better, doctor Chiang or me?" She replied. "How could he compare with you? You are Heaven. He is only a brick. You are above the thirty-three levels of Heaven. He is under the ninety-nine layers of earth. Without mentioning all your qualities, such as generosity, riches, and eloquence, you wear silk of the best quality, walk with three followers and sit with five servants. You are the master of other human beings. Only to mention what you eat and use in your everyday life—all of these valuable things, he would never have been able to see them, even if he had lived in this world for several centuries. How could he be comparable to you? You are the balm of my life. Since I have known you, I think of you from morning till night." These words made Hsi-men Ch'ing extremely happy. (1:19:458)

Hsi-men's question presumes a certain answer, and P'ing-erh has no other choice but to provide the expected answer by recognizing his superiority. He asks his question after having forced her, by beating her, to confront the immense disproportion between them—that is, the physical difference between a strong man and a weak woman. After describing to her the dirty trick he played on her ex-husband, he also confronts her with the social difference between an official and a widow longing for marriage.

Li P'ing-erh understands her situation perfectly well. In contrast to her usual reserve, she answers this question with remarkable volubility. She knows what she has to do to save herself: she resorts to flattery and exaggerates Hsi-men's wealth and power, including his sexual potency. For, as master in his household, Hsi-men has institutionalized the principle that his own pleasure takes precedence over anything else as the primary criterion of judgment.

He is not, however, totally ignorant of the limits of this principle. He understands quite well that those mightier than himself make their own demands for pleasure and that he must accommodate them. He has no choice but to acknowledge this reality. For example, when he is visited by the Imperial Censor Ts'ai he must provide his guest with money, good food, and two singing girls. The censor can satisfy his every desire without having to ask for a thing.

To this extent, Hsi-men understands at least one very important truth: in order to preserve his own kingdom of pleasure, he must learn how to obey the whimsical desires of other more powerful figures. This, again, resembles a market principle—a market of exchange of pleasure and power. Each degree of pleasure has its price, payable in social power.

As a result, he is not interested in what his partners truly think about him, as long as his victims openly acknowledge his authority. To a large extent, his sexual perversities are designed to prove his incontestable power; that is, his lovers are *unable* to contest it, not that they are *unwilling* to contest it. The will of Hsi-men's lover must be completely obliterated by his "dictatorship." One example can be seen in his predilection for burning incense on the bodies of his partners, which he successively performs on Wang Liu-erh, the wife of a servant; Madame Lin, a rich widow; and also Ju-yi, a maid.

By chance, a salesman employed by Han Tao-kuo, Liu-erh's husband, peeks through a crack of the wall, when Hsi-men burns incense on the body of his boss's wife.

> After quite a while, he heard the woman's voice. "My dearest father, if you want to burn incense on me, please choose any part you like. I dare not stop you. I am a whore whose

body belongs to you. I really don't care." Hsi-men answered, "I am afraid that your husband will be displeased." She said, "That turtle? [12] Does he have seven heads and eight bellies of guts? How dare he be displeased! He has to remember on whom he relies to make a living." (4:61:12)

The act of burning incense becomes a ritual of sexual domination. In each case, the burned spots are symbols of possession. Not only the woman, but even her husband has to prostrate himself before the same power, which is first of all economic—as in "on whom he relies to make a living." To this extent, the worship of sexual power is a worship of money.

The suffering of the woman extends the pleasure of Hsi-men. The burning spot on the woman's body becomes identified with the man's loss of semen—both symbols of a partial death—which unifies two discontinuous individuals in an act of violence. At the same time, this union paradoxically implies a distancing because it is founded on a total denial of the woman's will.

The passivity of a female partner in regard to her own suffering elevates Hsi-men to the position of absolute master. The body of the woman is turned into an incense burner like that with which believers ordinarily show their respect to Buddhas in a temple. In fact, Hsi-men's lovers behave even more "piously" on the sexual altar, since what is burnt is not a symbol but literally their own bodies. The cult of the sexual master is, then, unlimited for the entire human being is transformed into a single emblem. The human body in this sense is similar to the sacrificial animal destined to prove the power of the gods through its suffering.

In this sense, Hsi-men is not so distant from the French libertines in Laclos's novel. Yet there is an essential difference. The element of power that interests the libertines in *Les Liaisons dangereuses*—even in the case of a concrete power such as the possibility of lovemaking—is the psychological aspect—that is, the willing acceptance of his or her domination by his or her victim. But for Hsi-men Ch'ing, symbolic power—such as the worship of his absolute authority—must be materialized by these spots of burnt flesh.

To a large extent, the psychological power enjoyed by the French libertines in *Les Liaisons dangereuses* can be considered a by-product of the Christian notion of consciousness. In the Christian tradition, the self being a broken image of God, becomes an object that is worthy of study.

In Rousseau's novel as well as in a poetic tradition of spiritual love, this poeticized and romanticized "self" tends to replace the image of God as the object of worship. However, Laclos's transgression of the preromantic self is largely determined by the tradition of the transmutation between spiritual and worldly love in which medieval courtly love takes roots.

Conversely, Confucianism is more concerned with the concrete aspect of the relationship between "name" and "substance"—that is, adjusting one's behavior in accordance with one's name in the sense of the definition of individual identities by a given society. Having no strong faith in paradise, the Chinese tended to attach more importance to their name as the only means of existing after physical death.

Hsi-men's self-image does not possess any "psychological" depth. What he requires from his partners is not the worship of "soul" but merely the worship of "name"—the idolatry of appearance. It is not his partner's love that he seeks but her verbal recognition of his absolute authority, even if he knows that she is lying.

Indeed, he is sometimes willing to dictate the verbal recognition, as in his relationship with Ju-yi (whose maiden name is Chang Ssu-erh), the former wet nurse of his short-lived son.

> Hsi-men shouted, "Chang Ssu-erh, you whore, whose wife are you?" The woman replied, "I am your wife, master." Then, Hsi-men taught her. "You should say that you were once Hsiung Wang's wife, but today belong to your father." The woman repeated, "I was Hsiung Wang's wife, but today belong to my father." (4:78:706–07)

In other words, Ju-yi cannot choose between her husband and Hsi-men, but can only be chosen by the most powerful of the two. Acknowledging that she belongs to Hsi-men is tantamount to acknowledging his power. But this acknowledgment is meaningful only through comparison. Therefore, Hsi-men is not satisfied by her first statement. He must have the verbal recognition of the transaction of "property" by the "property" itself. By making Ju-yi repeat his own words, Hsi-men reduces his partner to an instrument of his power, which, in turn, is exercised on that very "instrument." Her speech no longer reflects her thought, but becomes an echo of her master's.

Since the recognition of his absolute authority is based on material power and violence, as soon as these two weapons are no longer intact after his death, it is natural that those women withdraw their respect. In this regard, the novel remains mercilessly realistic.

Sometimes, Hsi-men's relationships may emphasize his identification with a third party. The best example is provided by his relationship with the widow of a noble family, Madame Lin. It is the symbolic power of the dead husband that attracts him to the middle-aged woman in the first place.

In Hsi-men's first pilgrimage to Madame Lin's mansion, we can see through his eyes that the imposing presence of this house forms a clear contrast to the atmosphere of his own. (4:69:298–99) The very silence in the mansion imposes respect, especially as Hsi-men's own house teems day and night with the noise of music and endless quarrels.

The mansion is like an immense labyrinth. In his residence, however, even the grotto in the garden, which seemingly provides the only hideaway, reveals the most fateful secrets of the lovers: they are always interrupted, sometimes even by animals, or spied on and overheard by hostile persons.

The contrast between his own mansion and the Lin family makes Madame Lin's mysterious image even more impressive for the hero. Moreover, this image is, for the moment, reinforced by the distance between Hsi-men and the woman, which is no less artificially maintained. Given that her secret is no longer intact—even to the singing girls—her discretion appears more ritualized than practical. The facade of ritual creates the impression of depth, as if behind it were something unknown, hidden, and mysterious.

After a long and complicated journey, Hsi-men finally reaches Madame Lin's apartment. But instead of coming face-to-face with his idol, who, like a goddess, can see without being seen, he sees the portrait of the man who has created the symbolic power of this mansion. On the wall, there is a couplet in gold and with elegant calligraphy which reads, "The inherited virtue in the family remains as evergreen as pine trees and bamboos. The heroic exploits on behalf of the nation are as everlasting as the Mount T'ai." (4:69:299)

The narrator emphasizes the emptiness of name through the irony in the couplet. Gold and beautiful calligraphy cannot hide the discrepancy between the glorious names of the past generation and the shameful behaviors of the present family members. "The inherited virtue" is mercilessly belied by both mother and son because their misdeeds are the very opposite of the prescriptive behaviors of the name which they inherited from their ancestors.

Naturally, Hsi-men himself is unable to appreciate the ironic undertone of this situation, for irony is not his favorite trope. On the contrary, he is plunged into near ecstatic admiration for the imposing decoration in the house, until a bell sounds to interrupt his revery.

On the other side of the world, hidden behind the curtain, the aristocrat Madame Lin peers out at our parvenu hero, not without her own feelings of strong admiration. The narrator thus intensifies irony in this contradiction between name and reality, for what she admires in our hero is actually his ostentatious wealth (five lines of golden buttons), his power (his "cunning" physiognomy, which reveals a useful skill in gaining power in the political intrigues of his time), and his sexual potency (by learning that after P'ing-erh's death he still has five wives).

One may say that Madame Lin and Hsi-men represent two different aspects of power: the former enjoys a privileged name, and the latter, a material advantage. As Hsi-men prostrates himself in front of the powerful name of her husband, at the same moment she secretly covets the substantial benefits of being the wife of a parvenu.

Despite René Girard's argument,[13] one need not necessarily have a Christian education to desire the forbidden fruit. Since the desire of possession is unlimited but the possibility of its realization remains limited, what one cannot possess always seems to be better than what is already in one's possession—in accordance with the economic principle of scarcity. In this sense, desire is a fiction that needs to be generated or at least maintained by desire of others.

The possession of Madame Lin is, for Hsi-men, symbolic of acquiring new power. It is, at the same time, a battle between two different forces: symbolic and actual powers.

To a certain extent, one may identify the symbolic power with Confucian ethics, the basis of hierarchical society, whereas the actual power originates in a denial of this moral structure, supported by practical values such as money. The *Chin P'ing Mei* is a worldly book to the extent that neither "name" nor "ideal" can ever, even for a short moment, prevail over practical interests in the human world.

When he burns Madame Lin's body with incense after sexual intercourse, Hsi-men enacts his possession, hence the triumph of "substance" over "name." But this triumph can only be temporary, since this attainment of the height of his power marks the eve of his death. Later on, the detachable name of Lin's defunct husband will continue to function, whereas Hsi-men's actual power will disappear with his person.

Numberless and Nameless

In a large number of Western novels of the "realistic" tradition, the fate of the hero, or heroine according to Lukacs, is to struggle against his or her limitations. Even though the battle is doomed from the beginning, the hero or heroine still persists to the end; it is precisely this stubbornness that makes the role and the character coherent.[14]

What makes Hsi-men utterly different from such Western dreamers (including Merteuil and Valmont) is that he is not really concerned with his limitations. The "philosophy of life" of this Chinese hero is to satisfy as much as possible his immediate desires within this world. Without desire and gratification, there is, for him, only unnameable blankness—"unnameable" not in the sense of an obscure profundity, but in the sense of shallowness.

Hsi-men can name his desire only through its concrete object, never abstractly. When the object has lost its *raison d'être* after the short-term conquest, so, too, does his desire become empty and unnameable. To a certain degree, this lifelong quest for unlimited gratification is, in the end, nothing but emptiness.

As his fifth wife, P'an Chin-lien, states in her characteristically colorful language:

> Salt is salty everywhere, just as vinegar is always sour. . . .
> If you had followed your own desire, you would have made love with all the women in this world. (4:61:18)

In *The Golden Lotus*, the effort to understand someone else is usually motivated by practical considerations. The quality of "penetration," which plays a central role in the game of the French libertines in *Les Liaisons dangereuses*, does not have much impact on the Chinese characters in *The Golden Lotus*. In Wang P'o's analysis of Hsi-men's possible adultery with Chin-lien at the beginning of the novel, not a single word is mentioned by the matchmaker about Chin-lien's personality; every sentence concerns how women in general react in similar circumstances.

Psychological elements are, like anything else, a means by which to reach a goal, but the means itself is not important in the Chinese context. Chin-lien's perception of her husband provides us with a good example. Her description is accurate but superficial. What troubles her is the result of Hsi-men's behavior: she has to share her husband, not only with the other wives, but also with his numerous lovers.

If Chin-lien often surmises Hsi-men's thoughts accurately, this is also because the two share the same strong craving for sexual pleasure and neither is interested in any moral standard. Like most of the other characters in this novel, she, too, can understand others only in terms of her own desire.

Whenever Hsi-men expresses a sentiment that differs from her own—his mourning for P'ing-erh, for example—she, more than anyone else, is at a loss to understand it. Chin-lien is surprised because she is incapable of feeling strongly about anyone, neither her husband nor her mother. As long as she has someone to sleep with, no death is too great a loss. As she expresses her surprise at Hsi-men's insatiable longing for new lovers, she again fails to understand Hsi-men's motivation.

Even though Hsi-men Ch'ing and P'an Chin-lien share the same kind of insatiable sexual desire, they face society from different perspectives. As a woman, Chin-lien does not have too much opportunity for adventures. For her, any man who can satisfy her physical desire is considered "salt" or "vinegar"—with the possible exception of her first dwarf husband whose ugliness is somehow beyond measure.

By contrast Hsi-men Ch'ing, as a rich and powerful man, has a much larger number of choices. "Salt" or "vinegar" is no longer sufficient. Nevertheless, Hsi-men's longing for diversity does not aim for quality but quantity.

Since psychological factors do not occupy a place of importance in the way Hsi-men Ch'ing differentiates between women, the flesh is overwhelmingly important. But it is difficult to distinguish one body from another based only on physical differences. Without quality, quantity is, in essence, reduced to a single object; conquest, then, consists in endless repetition.

It is like a vicious circle: the more Hsi-men moves from one object to the next, the more he needs to have some conquests to overcome his sense of emptiness. The more he accelerates his successive conquests, the less he is satisfied. The objects become more and more alike, as the women completely lose their respective identities.

For example, Madame Lin's family background seems to distinguish her from the others. But, once the hero succeeds in putting her in the position of Wang Liu-erh by burning incense on her body, his victory also spells his failure, since the mark of his domination on her body abolishes her own mark of distinction.

Chang Chu-p'o, the traditional commentator on the book, is probably right in saying that "festivity" (*Ch'ing*),[n] Hsi-men's first name, implies the notion of emptiness through its homonym "void" (*ch'ing*).[o] In other words, Hsi-men's life seems to be composed of "festivity," but, in reality, "emptiness" remains its fundamental nature.

The longing for diversity in a sense joins Hsi-men to Valmont, the French libertine in *Les Liaisons dangereuses*. Both yearn for change. But what Valmont hopes to find in Tourvel, his devout lover, is his own image of uniqueness, which is primarily a qualitative difference. On the other hand, Hsi-men is more interested in quantitative difference in changing his lovers ceaselessly. Even though the case of Li P'ing-erh, his sixth wife, apparently presents an exception, Hsi-men himself cannot perceive this as a qualitative difference, except by translating his longing for her as gustatory desire or financial concerns.

It is Hsi-men's unrestricted desire that brings about his own destruction, as prefigured by the death of P'ing-erh, his favorite wife. After taking medicine given by the phallic Indian monk, he insists on making love with her while she happens to be menstruating. In traditional China, people believed that sexual intercourse during the menstrual period might cause misfortune to the man and severe sickness to the woman—even death.[15]

Although P'ing-erh repeatedly refuses him and tries to send him to Chin-lien's house with the intention of preserving her health and calming the jealous wife, Hsi-men thinks only about his immediate desire and disregards P'ing-erh's concern. In the end, Hsi-men even takes an oath to his wife in order to beg her:

> Tonight I don't know why, I only want to sleep with you. Well, how about letting me beg you for this favor. (3:50:505)

Even though P'ing-erh greatly fears undermining her health and her relationships with others, Hsi-men's last gesture of supplication leaves her no choice but to obey him.

The object of Hsi-men's desire is the here and now; it is difficult for him to postpone the fulfillment of desire unless the circumstances absolutely preclude it. Since he can only conceive of objects of desire as a function of the fulfillment of his own instincts, and he cannot worry too much how to preserve the objects, his desire is necessarily destructive. He never makes any connection between his own behavior and its disastrous results, because he immediately forgets what happened before.

Later on, P'ing-erh, indeed, dies of a hemorrhage, which was considered to be a consequence of sexual intercourse during menstruation. Hsi-men, however, never makes the connection. The present very often exists as an isolated moment for the hero of this Chinese novel who has neither regret for the past nor concern for the future.

His lovers—mostly the wives of his servants—are more attractive to him for two reasons: first the relationships with them make him feel superior to their pitiful husbands; and second, he does not need to finalize the relationships in marriage. To a large extent, the hero needs the figure of the husband—mostly absent—to enjoy his relationship with a woman. A husband—normally a rival—is, in fact, Hsi-men's helper by intensifying his desire and sparing him from further consequences. This partially explains his relative indifference toward innocent girls.[16]

At the end of his life, Hsi-men will eventually yearn for women to whom he has almost no access—such as the wives of Wang San-kuan and He Ch'ien-hu, two men who, despite their youth, can be considered his equals in rank even though both of them are, in one way or another, his protégés. The former, following instructions of his adulterous mother, becomes his adopted son; the latter, due to connections between his uncle, the Eunuch He, and the hero, becomes, in a sense, his pupil. But both of them possess an advantage that is lacking to Hsi-men: they are from powerful and influential families.

The rivalry with Wang San-kuan in respect to the singing girls provides a good example. Regardless of Hsi-men's money and power, not only is his first singing girl, Li Kuei-chieh, always attracted to this pampered son, but so, too, is his favorite, Ai-yüeh-erh, who also obviously has relationships with him. She has his calligraphy and painting in her bedroom and knows his recent change of *hao*[p]—a detail seemingly known only by a few intimate friends.[17] Moreover, the reader of *The Golden Lotus* cannot escape an awareness of the importance of puns in names. Hsi-men's *hao* is "The Fourth Fountain" (*Ssu-ch'üan*);[q] and his adopted son's is coincidentally "the Third Fountain" (*San-ch'üan*).[r] Thus, he becomes the older brother of the pretended father.

In the Confucian tradition, "name" is not simply taken as a sign, but as a moral or political rule, according to which the one who is so named must behave properly. Therefore, Confucius in his lifetime devoted much energy to the "rectification of names" (*cheng ming*).[s] Confucius says:

> If names be not correct, language is not in accordance with the truth of things, affairs cannot be carried on to success. When proprieties and music do not flourish, punishments will not be properly awarded. When punishments are not properly awarded, the people do not know how to move hand or foot.[18]

What one must respect in a name is not an unapproachable, far-reaching truth, but the act of naming within society which is reflective of social order.

For Confucius, the art of governing a country can be summarized in eight characters:

> Prince [must act as a] prince; minister [as a] minister; father, [as a] father; son, [as a] son. (*chün-chün, ch'en-ch'en, fu-fu, tzu-tzu*).[t]

If everyone were to act in accordance with the principles indicated by one's name, society would be in perfect order.

Following the same pattern, to disregard names means to transgress social order. Names require unconditional recognition as well as total acceptance. To question the validity of a name is worse than transgressing a political law of a government or an economic law of a society, since both of them are based on the very authority of names. The hero of *The Golden Lotus* in many ways undermines the basis of the naming system by using "unrectified" or "unjustified" names.

Hsi-men Ch'ing has a large number of adopted relatives who are bound to him, not by blood lineage, but by names. In all these relationships, the act of naming is motivated by the three objects of his desire: money, power, and sex. From the Confucian point of view, the basis of these names is initially unjustified. One example can be seen in the father-and-son relationship between Ts'ai Ching and the hero.

The former is a corrupt prime minister, famous for his evil doings in the Sung Dynasty. In order to ensure the protection of this powerful figure, Hsi-men wants to become his adopted son. He reaches this end with the help of his money and of his relationship with Chai Ch'ien who readily influences the decision of the prime minister as the favorite manager of his household.

Hsi-men also has an apparent family tie with the manager, in a loose sense—namely, Chai's marriage with his "child." But in reality, the relationship between the hero and Chai's concubine can be said to be much deeper.

Taking into account that the concubine's mother is Wang Liu-erh, one of his favorite lovers, one may consider Hsi-men as a sort of stepfather of the concubine, except that this name is "unnameable." In short, Hsi-men provides the manager with a beautiful girl from his household in the name of his own daughter, in exchange for the protection of Chai's master in the name of his father. In both cases, the motivation of naming is not "justified."

In traditional China, even if the name is not "justified," the relationship implied by that name is no less subject to transgression. Once a relationship is named legitimately or by accident, the one who is named must behave as one bound by blood lineage. For example, an adopted son ought to venerate his named father, and the latter should love the former as if there were no difference between this named relationship and that of blood.

In Hsi-men's case, the unjustified names are very often motivated by a desire to facilitate his sexual relationships. In this sense, "name" is doubly profaned by the initial act of naming and by the following incestuous act. For example, he is very angry at Wang San-kuan, Madame Lin's pampered son because of the latter's flirtation with Li Kuei-chieh, the singing girl kept with a monthly pension by Hsi-men. In order to take revenge, the hero wants to commit adultery with Wang's beautiful wife who is neglected by her lighthearted husband.

Hsi-men starts by courting the mother, Madame Lin, whose sexual hunger is somehow expected to facilitate his eventual relationship with the daughter-in-law. At the same time, Madame Lin urges her son to become Hsi-men's adopted son to facilitate her own adultery. Here, the father-and-son relationship is predicated on sexual rivalry concerning prostitutes and the conjugal bed.

Taking into account the seriousness with which the Chinese treated names in traditional society, Hsi-men's relationships with Wang's family are incestuous on various levels. In short, the hero violates a strongly organized center of Chinese culture in transgressing the integrity of names. In turn, he undermined the naming system which entails the dispersal of another ethical center, that of family unity.

In any case, Hsi-men is not completely indifferent to names. One good example is provided by his relationship with Madame Lin, the middle-aged widow who no longer offered any attractions except her insatiable sexual hunger and the tarnished name of her dead husband. However, a symbolic dimension is never sufficient for our hero and must be always accompanied by the presence of the flesh. The middle-aged widow replaces her youthful daughter-in-law in this respect, just as the far less attractive body of an anonymous servant substitutes for another unreachable woman, Lan-shih who is He Ch'ien-hu's wife and for whom Hsi-men's sexual urge will literally cause his death.

Wang San-kuan is somewhat weaker than Hsi-men since, protected only by the name of his ancestor, he himself is not a high official. In this sense, his wife is less inaccessible to Hsi-men than is Lan-shih, who apparently also has a more stable relationship with her husband. The latter is not only equal in terms of official position but also superior in terms of political connections with the court, not to mention his younger age which is an advantage both in career and in sentimental life. Hsi-men has to struggle very hard to become an official when he is in his late thirties, whereas this young man easily obtains the same position in his early twenties through the connections of his powerful uncle of whom he is the only heir.

In this sense, Lan-shih's attraction stems, not only from her youthful beauty, but also from her position within a social context that is beyond Hsi-men's reach. The narrator describes his meeting with Lan-shih sarcastically.

> It would have been all right, if Hsi-men had not seen her. But from the moment he saw her, his soul flew beyond the heavens, his spirit has completely dispersed. He ejaculated semen without any physical contact. A moment later, Yüeh-niang and the others greeted her and introduced her in the rear hall so that they went out to meet everyone. After the formal introduction, they invited Hsi-men to meet her. Hsi-men was so impatient that with a word of reply he hurried up to salute the visitor. She appeared vaguely like the jade tree of the heavenly forest descending in the mortal world and like the goddess of Wu Mountain coming down in his dream. He made a bow, with his heart shaken, his eyes floating, losing all self-control. (4:78:732)

The expression "soul flying and spirit dispersed" (*hun-fei p'o-san*)[u] usually describes a situation of extreme fright in which the subject is surprised by a great danger. Here, it results from an extreme desire that is not so different from the former: both situations carry the possibility of death.

The loss of sperm prefigures Hsi-men's loss of life. Instead of observing the woman with a clear gaze, Hsi-men sees her only dimly, as would a person on his deathbed, more because of his dizzy consciousness than because of her dreamlike beauty.

The second simile—of a goddess—points both to the dimension of dream and to the aspect of sexual frenzy. In Sung Yü's "Rhapsody of Kao-t'ang" *kao-t'ang fu*, the Prince of Ch'u dreamed of a beautiful goddess and made love with her. Afterward, the goddess told the prince that she became a floating cloud every morning and rain on the river every evening. Since then, "cloud and rain" have become, in Chinese, an expression for sexual intercourse. Moreover, because it only lasted a moment, it always implies a certain ephemeral nature.[19] Hsi-men's desire for endless possession can only be a dream, which, with his life, is soon to be dispersed like the "clouds and rain" on Wu Mountain. One may also say that the entirety of his life is composed of "clouds and rain" in its double sense.

For example, Miao Ch'ing, the criminal servant, thanks to Hsi-men's support, murdered his master and married his wife with impunity. In order to thank Hsi-men, Miao provides him with a beautiful singing girl, named the "Cloud of Ch'u," (*Ch'u-yün*),[v] alluding to the same legend. Indeed, this beautiful singing girl disappears like a cloud before Hsi-men even has a chance to meet her. She becomes Lan-shih's double in the sense of being the object of an unfulfilled desire.

The last two expressions in the description of his meeting with Lan-shih, "heart shaken" and "eyes floating" portray the predicament of a dying person who has lost control of both body and mind. Indeed, Hsi-men's desire for this unattainable woman becomes the cause of his death. Hidden behind the door curtain, he peers at Lan-shih who is leaving his house at the end of the banquet.

> His eyes expressing craving almost penetrated darkness, and he could hardly hold back saliva, itching for intercourse with her. (4:78:734)

The briefness of the meeting between the hero and Lan-shih intensifies his longing to the point that it is seemingly transformed into a passion, a flame. As Derrida describes it:

> The fact that, cut off from any ultimate, "real" reference— which would keep the fire at a reassuring distance—this sort of consumption seems to consume only traces, ashes, and to shed light on nothing that would be present, in no way prevents it from burning. . . . Like the crime, this consumption or consummation never "really" takes place. It hovers between desire and fulfillment, perpetration and remembrance.[20]

Lan-shih, the distinguished and youthful woman, represents the "real" object of desire "at a reassuring distance," precisely because of her inaccessibility and unreality. But instead of longing for the "ultimate reference" of a metaphysical world, Hsi-men turns toward the empirical world, incarnated by the bodies of some other women which are much more tangible than that of the object of his desire.

Immediately after the banquet and still excited by his colleague's beautiful wife, he engages in frantic intercourse with a servant whom he hardly knows anything about, not even her name. Then, he goes to Wang Liu-erh's house—the one he has bought recently for her and her husband—to make love with her.

> Hsi-men Ch'ing thought only about Lan-shih, the wife of He Ch'ien-hu. His desire was as intense as if it were burning, and his private parts remained erect. (4:79:746)

He is consumed by a desire of what is absent; but "traces," "ashes" that are burned in the place of the absent object are the flesh and blood of human bodies. Between the signifier—the bodies of other women—and the signified—Lan-shih's body— there is no qualitative difference because the substitute and the substituted here belong to the same category. What distinguishes the one from the other is, rather, the degree of degradation in terms of social position, age, and beauty.

These differences are amplified and intensified in the eyes of Hsi-men by the distinction between the unreachable body and the tangible flesh. In other words, only absence can nourish and maintain a long-term desire, represented by the image of his penis which remains continually erected from this point to the end of his life. The same flame, which consumes the flesh of his lovers as signifiers of the unattainable object, ends up burning out Hsi-men's own body through the "signifier of desire," the phallus. As Jacques Lacan explains:

> For the phallus is a signifier, a signifier whose function, in the intrasubjective economy of the analysis, lifts the veil perhaps from the function it performed in the mysteries. For it is the signifier intended to designate as a whole the effects of the signified, in that the signifier conditions them by its presence as a signifier.[21]

In fact, the Chinese novel excels in graphic descriptions of this organ, the signifier of the desire of the Other. After Hsi-men reveals his temptation to seduce P'an Chin-lien, his fifth wife-to-be, to the old matchmaker, she tells him that the dimension of his penis—together with money, beauty, patience, and leisure—comprises the indispensable conditions of a successful affair (1:3:63–64).[22]

Later on, the physiognomy of the Indian monk who gives Hsi-men the philter—this monk, with his runny nose, his dress, the color of flesh, his soft neck, and his sanguine skin—is described as a phallus. (3:49:223) If we exclude external factors, such as money and power, Hsi-men's phallus, to a large extent, incarnates his desirability in the eyes of his sexual partners.

His sixth wife, Li P'ing-erh, for example, is personally richer than Hsi-men Ch'ing. While her first husband is not as cunning as Hsi-men in taking advantage of political intrigues to gain power, she herself does not lack personal connections with certain political figures. P'ing-erh's short-lived second marriage to the apparently more solicitous and stable doctor, Chiang Chu-shan, is unsuccessful, not necessarily for want of money or power but because of his relatively weaker sexual potency. Although the poor doctor tries to please her with all kinds of instruments, he cannot satisfy Li P'ing-erh after she has experienced the "hard blowing wind and torrential rain" (*k'uang-feng chou-yü*)[w] (1:19:440) in the bed of master Hsi-men.

In this sense, the phallic monk who provides Hsi-men with the magic potion is the source of Hsi-men's desirability. By his physical appearance and his function, the monk can be said to be an icon of Hsi-men's phallus, on which the desires of his lovers seem to converge. As Lacan describes,

> The fact that the phallus is a signifier means that it is in the place of the Other that the subject has access to it. But since this signifier is only veiled, as ratio of the Other's desire. . . .[23]

In fact, his desirability, or his sexual potency, functions also as a means of exchange. The Indian monk says,

> "[The potion] is so valuable that it is neither exchangeable for nor measurable by gold or jade." (3:49:229)

As Derrida indicates:

> "In all things excess is a defect". . . . In the same way, the trace can only trace itself out in the erasure of its own "presence," so that tracing is not simply the mere other or outside of erasing. Scription contra-diction. Number, the trace, the frame—each is at once itself and its own excess facing [*débord*].[24]

The philter that the monk bestows on Hsi-men seemingly allows him to satisfy completely the desire of his own desirability and at the same time leads to its fatal overflowing. As the source of a surplus of energy, the portion also carries with it the element of death. Li P'ing-erh's death prefigures Hsi-men's ending, not only in terms of causality—both due to the use of the philter or, more precisely, of the intense desire excited by the philter—but also in terms of form.

P'ing-erh's exhausting bleeding, for example, is no different from Hsi-men's complete loss of semen. Both are dead because of the effects of draining.[25] In this sense, the phallus, which is the signifier of excessive desire, becomes, in the end, the signifier of emptiness, death, and dissemination.

3

Language of Love:
Love for Language

Les *Liaisons dangereuses* and *The Golden Lotus* form a cross-cultural pair in their ways of portraying the negative aspects of sexuality: destructive desire and domination. In a parallel manner, *Julie, ou la Nouvelle Héloïse*[1] and *The Dream of the Red Chamber*[2] are comparable in their descriptions of the positive aspect, which is sublimation of sexual desire.

As we have seen in the first two chapters of this book, the French libertines in Laclos's novel pay much more attention to a well-structured self-image than the Chinese hero in the erotic novel who is more preoccupied by his immediate desire. Similarly, St. Preux and Julie in *La Nouvelle Héloïse* describe their feelings self-consciously with a well-formulated rhetoric of love. In a sense, to express their mutual feelings in language is to conceptualize them.

By contrast, for Pao-yü and Tai-yü in *The Dream of the Red Chamber*, misunderstanding—manifested in the form of quarrel—paradoxically is one of the most important means, if not the only one, of communication and mutual understanding. In the Chinese literary tradition, rhetorically "lofty love" is not purified from "shameful lust" or physical desire in sexual relations. Even in *The Dream of the Red Chamber—the* Chinese novel of love—the distinction between "love" and "lust" is also linguistically ambiguous. Moreover, genuine love in the Chinese novel is not communicable in language. This is just the opposite of what we will see in Rousseau's novel in which love, to a large extent, exists only in language.

Love is primarily nostalgic in Rousseau's *Julie, ou La Nouvelle Héloïse*. By this, I mean that Julie and St. Preux, the two lovers in the novel, can enjoy passion only retrospectively. Further, in most cases, their past happiness does not necessarily accord with what "really" happened, but is a linguistic reinvention of the past through the present act of writing. The "past" feeling functions as a contrast to the present one, and, by highlighting the contrast, the two lovers often intensify their present unhappiness in order to appreciate their "past" happiness.

As a result, passion is a desire for *desire*, since it aims at its own unfulfillment in order to preserve itself in the act of writing. In fact, writing saves passion from the inconsistency and impurity of everyday life; it is a process of spiritualization. Needless to say, sensual experience hinders this process by materializing desire in a physical union. Spiritual love, in other words, needs to be created through a narrative act from the neutralization—or even the negation—of the present.

Each lover finds in the other the portrait of his or her own subjective world. In the end, what interests the lover in the beloved is no longer objective qualities but self-projection. By exalting the sublimity of the beloved, the lover who is the best "knower" of this quality becomes as if he or she is more sublime than the object of worship. Therefore, the elevation of the beloved allows the lover to establish the superiority of his or her own value system over social convention. Nevertheless, attendant on the sublimation of desire is also the domestication of the subversive force in passion, since the word "superiority" already implies the recognition of society.

Furthermore, even though social difference stands in the way of their love being accepted in society, the ways in which the lovers project the image of the self onto each other are also not without social prejudices. St. Preux, the commoner, must do something to "deserve" the affection of his beloved, whereas Julie, the noble woman, honors her lover by her simple presence in his heart.

This subtle asymmetry leads, in part, to Julie's marriage—the act of renouncing her love for St. Preux in this world. Their love remains sublime, partially because it does not actually break any social conventions. The desire that is sublimated is in the realm of dream not of reality. In the end, since both of them prohibit the consummation of passion or the realization of desire, the result of their "sublime passion" corresponds to the decision of Julie's father which is arbitrarily prescribed by his prejudices and the social hierarchy.

The worship of Julie is shared by both the lover and the husband—and, in a sense, by everyone living in Clarens. Julie's loving nature even moves the hearts of her servants, and, by virtue of that nature, she is mystified and divinized. This divinization is tantamount to reification, as Julie is an image onto which men can project their world of self with a relative freedom.

The margin of understanding left by mystification—which disallows realities—enables them to escape more easily from the constraints of a realistic image of the self. To be the knowers of her divine nature, they divinize their own images and ignore Julie's personal needs, which are hidden behind the image of her perfectly balanced nature.

From the point of view of the husband, Wolmar can peacefully enjoy *his own act* of saving his loving wife from the destructive effects of passion. From the point of view of the lover, St. Preux has reason to admire himself while admiring the "divine equilibrium" of his beloved. Both can live remorselessly without worrying too much about understanding this "divine nature,"—until Julie perishes from the hidden tension behind her apparent serenity.

Writing and Lost Paradise

In *Julie, ou la Nouvelle Héloïse* the lovers are always in love with their past, and condemning of their present. Happiness can only be reconstructed in language, as something existing in a past, distinct and remote from the empirical present. In this case, desire for the beloved is, first of all, a linguistic desire, or a "desire for desire."

Such desire must remain unsatisfied at an existential level so that it may be prolonged at the level of writing which "spiritualizes" desire by replacing its material object. In other words, the narrative success of love requires its failure at an experiential level. The object of spiritual love is a past forever lost, but reconstructed in language according to a certain remembered image. Its nature is essentially nostalgic.

As Claire writes to St. Preux in her letter:

> In my life I have never seen a lover so grumbling as you. You are always ready to argue over everything, and love for you is only a state of war; or if sometimes you are tractable, it is for the purpose of then complaining that you have been so. (2:8:182)

The first sentence comes from Molière's *Misanthrope*. Célimène says to Alcest, "One has never seen such a grumbling lover."[3] By identifying St. Preux and Alcest in the name of the "grumbling lover" (*amant grondeur*), Rousseau turns into a tragical feature Alcest's misanthropy, which is, in Molière's play, a rather comic feature.

This shift reveals a change in the relationship between the individual and society. Misanthropy is, by definition, the "hatred of society." A misanthrope is an individual who cannot fit in with his society. In neoclassicism, loneliness, unsociability, and excessiveness were objects of mockery. For Molière and his contemporaries, misanthropy was only a sickness or abnormality in a normative society. Alcest was an antihero as Misantrope, because the true hero is counter example, a well-balanced gentleman.

This situation has been gradually changed during the Century of Enlightenment. In Rousseau's novel, sincerity, even if it results in an impaired sociability, tends to replace moderation in the past century as an important virtue. Misanthropy is no longer a disease but a mark of distinction. Suffering gains a positive value because it distinguishes the individual from the world surrounding him. This change of attitude marks the transition from neoclassicism to preromanticism or to romanticism.

Indeed, St. Preux is never glad of the present situation. To a certain extent, the same can be said of Julie, who is no doubt more reserved and less plaintive. In this sense, both belong to the category of "grumbling lovers"—descendants of Molière's misanthrope. However, the one who is to blame for the divergence between the subjective and the objective worlds is no longer an individual but society as a whole.

In order to preserve the quality of "lovers," St. Preux and Julie have to keep "grumbling." If the external world does not offer any subject for complaint, the lovers complain about each other.

In the first two books, nobody seems to hinder the two lovers from enjoying pastoral love before the return of Julie's father. In fact, their mutual attachment—mistaken by Julie's mother for an innocent friendship that is favorable to her daughter's intellectual development—is even highly encouraged by the family. But Julie and St. Preux themselves, time and again, raise obstacles to their happiness by looking for subjects about which to quarrel.

As in *Les Liaisons dangereuses*, love is a battle. Secretly, the lovers also desire to fight. But they differ from Laclos's libertines in that their battle is fought against themselves—since the beloved is supposed to be the "other self" of the lover. A libertine like Valmont can proclaim his victory over Tourvel, because he conquers her heart as a trophy of victory. Rousseau's lovers, by contrast, have no true victory since their victory also signifies their own failure.

Therefore, the endless war is the best expression of their everlasting dissatisfaction. As St. Preux writes:

> Do not think that I have forgotten the rules imposed upon me nor lost the will to observe them. No, but a secret resentment disturbs me in seeing that these laws are painful only to me, that you who once pretended to be so weak are so strong at present, and that I have so few struggles to make against myself, so careful are you to prevent them. (1:8:40)

Love can be confirmed only by a painful struggle of the lover against himself or herself. Without this battle against the self, passion is futile or groundless. Because passion exists only in its difference from reality, suffering is its indispensable price. A lover has to struggle not only against social conventions, but also against laws created by himself or herself in accordance with social conventions, as well as against himself or herself—as if this were for creating an occasion of suffering. The hero states in the same letter:

> Tell me, tell me, you inconstant creature, is this the character of a violent, ungovernable passion? And if you had the slightest desire to conquer it, would not the constraint at least stifle your playfulness? (1:8:41)

"A violent, ungovernable passion" (*une passion violente reduite à se combattre à elle-même*) is a model for their love, a model existing in literature. As in the case of Tristan and Iseult, passion implies violence—or death. In addition, the "character" of passion is primarily narcissistic, as the reflexive verb and pronoun suggest to us.

Because there is conquest involved here, love is a war which necessarily implies hatred. Moreover, since at stake is also a battle against oneself because of the narcissistic nature of love, passion has a masochistic undertone. Consequently, it is not surprising to see the lovers respectively desire the destruction of the other (for example 5:9:615) and their own deaths (St. Preux's long letter to Edouard, 3:21:263–65 and Julie's dramatic ending 6:21:396–404) at a given moment.

Thanks to the obstacles and sufferings very often created by the lovers themselves, their feelings fulfill the "character of passion" which has been defined by their literary tradition. In this sense, love is a product, not only of their writing, but also of their reading. The title of the book itself provides us with an excellent example. Love, haunted by past literary figures, must be associated with death and violence in order to fit its "character."

This secret desire for death is expressed in everyday-life situations by a search for suffering. Whenever St. Preux's past hopes are realized, the wish of the past becomes the object of his present sorrow. Conversely, the past sorrowful state becomes, in the present, the object of longing.

In the first letter, St. Preux complains about Julie's "cruel familiarity" (*familiarités cruelles*) (1:1:33), but when Julie changes this attitude, her past treatment is considered in his second letter "innocent familiarity" (*l'innocent familiarité*). (1:2:35) In a sense, the past is always "innocent," and the present, in one way or the other, is always "cruel." Happiness can exist only in narration which embellishes the bitterness and dissatisfaction of reality.

The function of language in *Julie, ou la Nouvelle Héloïse* is not primarily to give information about a real or fictitious reference, but to be a self-referential center or to create what is lacking in reality. In this, Rousseau is not all that distant from the medieval lyric tradition, in which the poetic language of unrequited love needs the failure of realization in the so-called "real world" to sustain itself.

Writing expresses desire, but the satisfaction of desire very often leads to the silence of writing.[4] In this case, the "desire for desire" is not the desire for the object but for its absence. Nevertheless, Rousseau differs from the troubadours or the writer of chivalrous romance in that his desire is expressed in an individualistic way, since the object of desire is a distinctive self-image. By contrast, in the case of medieval literature in general, the language of love seems more allegorical than personal.

In order to create this self-image, the desire for the beloved lady is necessarily fictional. In other words, it implies not only her presence, but also her absence, and not only her preservation, but also her destruction. In letter 3, St. Preux expresses his concern about Julie's health:

> At first I foresaw only the unhappiness of a hopeless passion that reason might overcome in time; next I became acquainted with a greater sorrow in the pain of displeasing you; and now I am experiencing the most cruel anguish of all in the discovery of your own misery. . . . Your bloom fades; an unusual pallor covers your cheeks; your gaiety leaves you; a mortal sadness overcomes you. . . . It is your recent sadness which has made me feel my own despair. (1:3:30)

The first three sentences mark chronologically the progress toward greater misfortunes. The misfortune that is the most distant from the present time is the least unbearable. This is a "no-way-out" situation: if the passion is unknown to the beloved, it is "hopeless" (*sans espoir*); if Julie learns of it, he feels anxious; and if the lady shares his feeling, his unhappiness is the most "cruel." In short, passion is, by definition, "hopelessly unhappy."

The following phrases contrast the past and the present as regards Julie's health: "bloom" (*vives couleurs*) versus "unusual pallor" (*pâleur étrangère*) in terms of physical appearance; and "gaiety" (*gaité*) versus "sadness" (*tristesse*) in terms of mental state. Progressive or oppositional, the change from the past to the present always implies a deterioration.

However, this deterioration is necessary for their passion, because the union of the two lovers can only be achieved negatively. In the last sentence of this passage, "your sadness" (*votre tristesse*) is identified with "my pain" (*mon mal*) through their common "progress" (*progresse*). Thanks to their unhappiness, the lovers are no longer postulated as subjects or objects of desire. They belong to the same world in their common nonfulfillment of desire.

In the same letter, St. Preux writes to Julie:

> For if I know myself, your happiness is dearer to me than my own. (1:3:30)

Here, he seemingly desires Julie's happiness, provided that he is not "mistaken himself" (*me trompe moi-même*). The problem is that he is forever "mistaken," because he needs to "cheat himself" (*tromper lui-même*) concerning the destructive nature of his passion in order to justify himself in his beloved's eyes as well as his own.

Several pages later, however, our hero changes his tone:

> Your languor has disappeared; there is no more mortification of despondency; all your graces have returned to their posts; all your charms are reanimated; the newly opened rose is not more fresh than you. . . . Oh, how much more amiable you were when you were less beautiful! How I miss that touching pallor, the precious assurance of the lover's

happiness, and how I hate the indiscreet health you have recovered at the expense of my tranquility! Yes, I should prefer to see you still ill rather than see this contented air, these brilliant eyes, this blooming complexion which outrages me. (1:8:40–41)

Again, St. Preux's desire for Julie's misfortune reminds us of Alcest in Molière's *Misanthrope*. Alcest, like St. Preux, desires the worst situation for his mistress so that he can become her only savior and the absolute master. For the preromantic novelist, this excessively possessive desire is a mark of distinction since it reveals St. Preux's sincerity. For the neoclassic playwright, however, the same excessiveness is ridiculed, because Alcest's similar desire does not fit the image of a moderate gentleman. Once again, the neoclassic antihero is turned into the preromantic hero in the name of "sensitive soul."

It would seem at first glance that what St. Preux desired with the most ardor in the preceding letter has been realized in the present. Julie is not only healthy again but also happy in loving him. But instead, her "happiness" (*bonheur*), which is "dearer than mine" (*plus cher que le mien*), "insults" (*outrage*) St. Preux. By contrast, the "mortal pallor" (*pâleur mortelle*) described in the preceding letter is now turned into the "touching pallor" (*pâleur touchante*), which is "precious guarantee of the lover's happiness" (*précieux gage du bonheur d'un amant*).

The situation is completely reversed. Julie's happiness is, indeed, "dear" for St. Preux, since her happiness costs his own peace. The symptom of her pain, this famous pallor, once it has disappeared, becomes the image of his happiness.

This does not necessarily mean that St. Preux is particularly sadistic, but that love and happiness are compatible only in the imagination while, in reality, love means suffering, be it mental or physical. To this extent, a realized dream is only a nightmare, whereas a past nightmare somehow manages to become the material of a beautiful wish.

Since writing can "spiritualize" desire by replacing its material object, one may say that spiritual love in Rousseau's novel is, first of all, textual pleasure. In this case, sensual pleasure, as the assertion of the union of the two lovers in the actual world, is the object of an ardent desire. At the same time, as the opposite of the spiritual, it is also the object of invincible fear. "Physical" is the antonym not only of "spiritual" but also of "linguistic," because its realization signifies the silence of language.

In the entire novel, only three scenes of sensual love are mentioned. In the scene of the "grove," it is the question of a simple kiss given to reward the self-control of the docile lover. Then, after Julie's sickness, the couple makes love for the first time, because Julie, feeling compassion for St. Preux's suffering, wants to change his emotional state by satisfying his physical desire. In the last of the three scenes, Julie uses sex as a strategy against the marriage imposed by her father.[5]

These three scenes have one point in common—physical love is not the end but a "supplément," to use Derrida's word, and an instrument through which the lovers try to attain another goal.[6] Instead of enhancing the existing situation, this "supplément" is doomed to worsen it and to occasion regret afterward.

After receiving the kiss, St. Preux writes to Julie:

> What have you done? Ah! What have you done, my Julie? You wanted to reward me and you have destroyed me. I am drunk, or rather, I am insane. My senses are disordered; all my faculties are disturbed by that fatal kiss. You wished to ease my pain? Cruel one, you sharpened it. It was poison that I gathered from your lips. It is seething within me, it inflames my blood it is killing me, and thus your compassion has caused my death. (1:14:52)

Julie's kiss is a gift, a generous "presence" that gives their love a physical presence. This reward of "sense" threatens to destroy St. Preux's self-control by making him "insane" (*insensé*) and "drunk" (*ivre*). To actualize love at a physical level is to "poison" both love and the lovers. The overflowing of physical sensation implies the loss of "sense" at a linguistic level and a consequent dissemination of the subject of love, since the meaning of "love" sustains itself best in a state of suspense, or "différance."[7]

At the end of the letter, St. Preux continues his complaints.

> A favor?. . . . It is a horrible torment. . . . No, keep your kisses, I cannot bear them. . . . They are too painful, too penetrating; they pierce, they burn to the quick. . . . They

would drive me insane. One, one only has thrown me into a frenzy from which I cannot recover. I am no longer myself, and you are no longer the same to me. (1:14:52)

It is true that in Western literary tradition, from *Aeneid* to *Tristan et Iseult*, to describe passion as "fire" or "wound" is almost commonplace. In many cases, passion seems very often to be excited by the impossibility of physical union. But here there is a difference between St. Preux's exclamation and that of his predecessors: the same expressions are used to describe frustration at the realization of a sensual experience and physical union—not the longing for it. The burns of kisses may express an irresistible passion, but, more likely, they are signs of a stinging feeling of regret *vis-à-vis* a prior state, now lost, of innocence. He is now "in a frenzy from which (he) cannot recover" (*dans un égarement dont je ne puis plus revenir*).

This feeling of an irreversible change or a fall is shared by Julie. While St. Preux complains about the kiss that has "thrown (him) into a frenzy from which (he) cannot recover," Julie uses the same turn of phrase after their first lovemaking in the scene of the grove. "I have fallen into the abyss of shame from which a girl never returns." (1:29:79)

The difference is that "frenzy" describes more the state of his "senses," but "abyss of shame" implies a certain normative social judgment. In other words, a man worries about himself, whereas a woman thinks about her image in the eyes of other people.

However, both emphasize that any return to the past is now impossible. Physical union, to this extent, is similar to human civilization in Rousseau's *Discours sur l'origine de l'inégalité parmi les hommes*.[8] Both destroy, once and for ever, the state of nature—or the earthly paradise—by intending to improve it.

Julie writes to St. Preux after their lovemaking:

There was a time, my dear friend, when our letters were easy and delightful. The sentiment which dictated them poured out with an elegant simplicity. They needed neither art nor coloring, and their purity constituted all their eloquence. That happy time is no more. Alas! It cannot return, and as the first consequence of so cruel a change, our hearts have already ceased to understand each other. . . .

That sweet enchantment of virtue is vanished like a dream. Our passions have lost that divine ardor which gave vigor to them by purifying them. We have sought pleasure, and happiness has fled us. Recall once more those delightful moments in which our hearts fused the more we respected each other, in which our passion drew from its own excess the strength to conquer itself, in which our innocence consoled us for our restraint, in which the homage paid to honor turned everything to the profit of love. (1:32:83–4)

Once again, language and feeling are analogical. The simplicity and clarity of writing equals to the innocence of feeling. As long as the sentiment is pure, writing is its perfect image. But sensual experience creates an obstacle, or a distance, which destroys this perfect analogy. The discrepancy between feeling and writing—the major mediator between the lovers—risks disturbing the symmetry between them. Thus, the sensual experience threatens the union of souls, or the very existence of spiritual love. Jean Baudrillard states:

The virtue of a word, its symbolic efficiency, is at the top while it is pronounced in emptiness, while it is without context and reference. It obtains force from a self-fulfilling. prophecy (or self-defeating prophecy).[9]

In *Julie,* the perfect union can exist only as a void or as a negation of real life that emerges from a language devoid of reference. Sensual love that substantializes the union and endows language with a reference necessarily destroys the "symbolic efficiency" of the sentimental discourse of the two lovers. The concretization of love demonstrates how great is the distance between language and reference, and between ideal and reality.

Ideal love remains self-sufficient, or a "self-fulfilling prophecy," precisely because its discourse is without reference. Language itself veils the world of the lovers; but sensual love unveils it and lays it bare. Julie states in the same letter:

We are nothing but common lovers. (1:32:84)

Physical experience forces the lovers to confront the real world which is neither simple nor pure. At the same time, this experience that embodies the discourse of love destroys the transparency of the signifier which exists, thanks to a zero degree of reference.

Julie's death provides an analogy: behind the Indian veil, which creates an atmosphere of sacredness, there is only the face of a dead body spoiled by heat. Physical experience is equal to unveiling the face of Julie in death; it ruins the mysterious charm of passion because sacredness, in both cases, remains in mystery. At the same time, the past, made sacred behind the veil of time, reproaches the lack of innocence of the present state. The existence of innocence is made sensible only by its absence.

By opposing "divine ardor" (*ardeur divine*) to sensual experience, Julie joins a long tradition off platonic lovers, reinforced by the emergence of Christianity in which the elevation of the soul requires the renunciation of the flesh. Since the body is sinful, the soul can be purified only by overcoming the temptation of its sinful residence. But in order to elevate itself, the soul needs, at the same time, the very passion that is the source of temptation. The lovers must accomplish an impossible task "in which our passion drew from its own excess the strength to conquer itself" (*où la passion tiroit de son propre excès la force de se vaincre elle-même*).

In this kind of battle, victory seems impossible since it simultaneously requires the spiritual expansion of passion and its physical restriction. But in fact, on one single condition victory is not only possible but also certain: it must occur in the past, as the "lost paradise" (*cela revient au même*), or in language as a fictional state, since the past is the material of fiction. In other words, passion gains or loses its values only tautologically since love, in Rousseau's novel, is primarily self-referential—a language of desire in which the object of desire is its own desirability.

The third scene, in which Julie uses sensuality as an instrument against the marriage arranged by her father, is no doubt the most successful one in terms of physical enjoyment. Never-

theless, the utmost pleasure is also the cause of external regret.
St. Preux declaims in a moment of ecstasy:

> What shall we do henceforward with an insipid youth, now
> that we have exhausted all its delights? . . . Withdraw those
> intoxicating favors for which I would give a thousand lives,
> but give me back all that does not depend upon them and
> surpasses them a thousand times. Give me back that inti-
> mate union of souls, which you had told me of and which
> you have made me enjoy so well. Give me back that languor
> so sweet, filled with the overflowing of our hearts; give me
> back that enchanting sleep found in your bosom; give me
> back that still more delightful instant of awakening, and
> those broken sighs, and those sweet tears, and those kisses
> that a voluptuous languor made us savor slowly, and those
> murmurs so tender, during which you pressed together
> those hearts which were made to be united. (1:55:123–124)

Although the passage is highly sensuous in tone, its sensuality is no more than the means to reach the "union of souls"
through which it is then purified and negated. As Starobinski
writes:

> The "false wisdom" of the world, which passion had de-
> nied, is substituted by a superior wisdom, originating in the
> same passion and clarified by the "repressive" disciplinary
> accepted with difficulties.[10]

These "intoxicating favors" (*ces faveurs enivrantes*) are physical gifts that St. Preux receives from Julie. Passion should be "intoxicating," but at the same time under control. In other words,
the "sensitive soul" does not simply follow its emotion. It has to
control its "senses." The "sensitive soul" must also be sensible; if
not, the "intimate union of souls" will disappear.

In the end, the gift of love should not be "intoxicating," but
rather the opposite, which helps the lover to suppress the overflowing of emotion. For St. Preux, the expressions of love which
he would like to preserve are subdued expressions. To a certain extent, the repression of passion is more enjoyable than its
fulfillment.

Sensuality, then, is purified by its own fire—passion. The most sensual experience is meaningful only in that it leads toward a fusion of hearts which, later on, allows the two lovers to renounce physical union. In the long run, what results from Julie's unconventional act coincides with what she intends to rebel against—namely, her father's arbitrary intention.

The passion that, in this scene, sublimates sexual pleasure makes any further physical union of the two lovers impossible. The essence of this intense enjoyment lies precisely in "that does not depend upon [it]." This "intimate union of souls" may be preserved only on the condition that physical pleasure is effaced. In this act of purification, Rousseau seems able to reconcile the irreconcilable—individual and society—by satisfying the former with imaginary freedom and the latter with concrete power of restriction.

It is significant that each sensual experience is immediately followed by the separation of the lovers. The third scene—which is the most fulfilling physically—ends in the accident caused by Edouard's generous but clumsy proposition to Julie's father with regard to the possible marriage of the two lovers. Following that, the two lovers will not see each other for several years—except for St. Preux's dramatic and hasty visit during Julie's sickness.

This separation is a sign of the failure of sensual experience, since the distancing that follows ensures that any further physical union is impossible; but, at the same time, it is a sign of its success since physical separation intensifies spiritual union—"union of souls"—through a crystallization of the past in the act of remembering and writing.

The past happiness, exalted in writing, to a large extent intensifies the present misfortune. As St. Preux describes the state of separation:

> Oh, absence! Oh, torment! Oh, bizarre and distressing situation, in which we can enjoy only the past moment and in which the present does not yet exist! (2:17:200)

Happiness, it seems, is never at hand. If the persons are not spatially separated, happiness is then temporarily separated from the present. It is not only embellished by memory but also, to a large degree, it is a product of memory. As Claire remarks:

> But what a curious whim, to leave you in order to have the
> pleasure of speaking of you! (4:9:298)

Spatial distance emancipates the imagination of the lovers
because their passion can then exceed the limits of reality. The
past itself is not happiness; it is only the material with which the
artistic imagination creates happiness, in contrast to its absence
in the present.

Change contributes both to creating the image of happiness
in the past and to deepening the feeling of misfortune in the
present. As St. Preux writes:

> What a difference—oh, Heaven—between those days, so
> charming and so sweet, and my frightful present misery!
> Alas! I was beginning to live and I sunk into nothing. The
> hope of life was warming my heart; now I have nothing be-
> fore me but the prospect of death. (2:1:159)

Love is enjoyable only if it can overcome mutability, but this
is doubly impossible. First, the lovers live in a changing world;
second, without change, they could never appreciate happiness
in love since happiness exists only in difference. In other words,
St. Preux's present "nothing" makes him aware of his past "existence," of the "prospect of death," and of the "hope of life."
The charms of the past are sufficiently appreciated only through
the "frightful misery" of the present.

However, the difficulty of remaining constantly in love in
this inconstant world appears insurmountable in the eyes of the
common people. Therefore, those who remain constant in their
passion are superior to the changing world. As St. Preux writes:

> Common people do not know violent sorrows, and great
> passions hardly develop in feeble men. (2:6:177)

But even the strong souls endowed with a passionate nature
sometimes regret the peaceful life without passion. St. Preux continues in the same letter:

> It is preferable never to have tasted happiness than to taste
> it and lose it. If I had been exempted from that fatal inter-

val, if I had evaded that first look which made another being of me, I should still be in possession of my reason, I
should still discharge a man's duties, and I should perhaps
show some virtues during my insipid career. A moment's
mistake has changed everything. My eye dared to look
upon what it was not supposed to see. That spectacle has
finally produced its inevitable result. After having been
gradually led to ruin, I am now only a fool whose mind is
deranged, a cowardly slave without courage who ignomini-
ously drags his chain and his despair. (2:1:159–60)

Before the fatal moment of meeting between the two beings
destined for each other by their inner similarity, the potential lovers, like the "*sauvages*" in his *Discours sur l'origine de l'inégalité
parmi les hommes*, live in an affectional situation parallel to the
state of nature.[11] They know neither felicity nor the chain of passion. The harmony they enjoy is based on lack of comparison, a
peaceful state of ignorance.

Leaving this prelapsarian state of innocence is brought
about by an accidental event beyond human control; it is the
crossing of a fatal interval which is forever irreversible.

Like their biblical ancestors, the lovers look at what they
were "not supposed to see," tasting what they should not even
touch. The same gesture forces both sides to learn about a new
world that they were condemned by divine or social law to ignore, and they fall into a state of lost innocence.

In spite of a long journey around the world, St. Preux has
not cured his passion. In order to avoid implications of adultery,
St. Preux writes to Julie's cousin, Claire, instead of Julie herself
who is now Mme. Wolmar and the mother of two children.
Moreover he uses the plural pronoun while he means only Julie:

I have circled the entire globe, and I have not been able to
escape you for a moment. We may try as we like to flee
from what is dear to us; its image, quicker than the sea and
the winds, follows us to the end of the universe, and everywhere we go we carry there what gives us life. (4:3:281)

But the incurable passion can be considered as already
cured in the sense that he is no longer in love with "what is dear

to us" but rather with "its image." The former is changeable, but the latter is "confined" "in the sanctuary." (6:7:675)

Wolmar, Julie's husband, is right in saying that St. Preux is in love with the memory of Julie, not her person. (4:14:329) Thanks to the function of memory, his love is, to a large degree, purified and liberated from physical desire. The comparison between the image and the person always works to the disadvantage of the latter, since the former remains the same—eternal—whereas the latter is always changeable—inconstant.

Furthermore, the essence of love lies in its narcissistic undertone. Later on, Julie, as the mother of two children, can no longer correspond to the perfect image which transcends St. Preux's self, even though their "hearts never cease from understanding each other." But her past image internalized in St. Preux's heart as "what gives us life" is the essence of his consciousness. The moment of meeting Julie accompanied by her two children accentuates this feeling:

> What did I become at this view? This can be neither told nor understood. A thousand cruel and delightful recollections came sharing my heart. Oh spectacle! Oh regrets! I felt torn by grief and transported by joy. I saw, so to speak, multiply the one who was so dear to me. Alas! I saw at the same moment the too vivid proof that she could no longer mean anything to me, and my loss seemed multiplied with her.[12]

To a certain extent, the present Julie becomes, at this moment, the image of her past. Her sons consist both of images of their mother and, at the same time, of the irrevocability of the past intimacy between the lovers. While in the past, St. Preux cherished Julie in his own imagination, now Julie herself becomes the living image of her past. The world surrounding her becomes another set of images—her children, her husband, her cousin, and even her servants.

For St. Preux, to live in Clarens is to surround himself with these kinds of images. But all these external images—changeable or not—are good only to the extent that they confirm his internal image—the image of the past Julie, of their common past, or rather of his "other self."

In preoccupying himself so deeply with the past, he sometimes neglects the present Julie, especially if she appears in conflict with her past image. In fact, the actual Julie may do damage to St. Preux's memory because she reminds her lover not only of her past, but also of her change from the past to the present. In this sense, her children and her household—including herself—are the image of changes. Therefore, St. Preux's sorrow is "multiplied" with the multiplication of Julie's present image.

In the same view, it is not surprising to read his exclamation: "Why isn't she dead!" (5:9:615)

Julie shares the same nostalgia. She describes their kiss in the grove under the eyes of her husband to her cousin:

> Alas! How wrong I should have been to make any! This kiss was nothing like the one which had made the grove fearful for me. I congratulated myself sadly for it, and I knew that my heart was more altered than I had dared believe it until then. (4:12:322)

Julie, it seems, has become what she wanted to become: a virtuous wife who treats her former lover decently—in a friendly but relatively indifferent manner. But the exclamation "Alas," the adverb "sadly" which forms an oxymoron with the verb "congratulate," and the negative form of the verb "dare" express the feeling of regret. The state that she consciously desired cannot be the source of joy, given that the realization of the same state is also the subject of fear.

This contradiction can be explained by the following reason: she is a social being but also an individual, and these two sides have opposing codes. The victory of the one is necessarily the defeat of the other. Again, a past is always the object of regret, because absence always makes the lost object more cherished than what is actually present. The lovers find themselves in a double bind: if there is no change, the coexistence of conflicting forces condemns them to live in a tension; if there is a solution, they regret what they have lost in the exchange.

Therefore, they live eternally in their "past happiness" and "present misery," precisely because true happiness has never existed either in the past or in the future. St. Preux describes his pilgrimage with Julie among the monuments of their past:

Those hundreds of little things which brought back the image of my past happiness—all returned to take a place in my memory in order to increase my present sorrow. It is over, I said to myself; those times, those happy times are no more. They have disappeared forever. Alas, they will return no more, and yet we live, we are together, and our hearts are ever joined! It seemed to me that I should have borne her death or her absence more patiently, and that I had suffered less the whole time I had spent parted from her. When far away I was aggrieved, the hope of seeing her again solaced my heart; I flattered myself that an instant in her presence would efface all my miseries. At least I used to envisage, out of all possible situations, one less cruel than my own. (4:17:338)

The actualization of an imagined situation in the present is also the condemnation of imagination, which eliminates illusion or hope, because the present situation is always the most "cruel" in St. Preux's eyes. In fact, deep within himself, he desires, more than anything else, the absence of the beloved because he can replace the "real" object of desire by his imaginative object more freely.

The object of desire becomes the obstacle of love, because Julie's presence limits her lover's love within this world. She is his hope only in her absence.

This logic leads the lover to contemplate murder and suicide in order to create an absolute absence or freedom *vis-à-vis* the restrictions of the present. At the same time, the author needs his characters' desperation in presence in order to "actualize" the language of his fictional world.

In the same vein, the possibility of describing love depends on the impossibility of experiencing it. The creation of *La Nouvelle Héloïse* itself points to its own principle of creation: the fortune of the novel is largely based on—or, more precisely, anticipates—the misfortune of the author's adventure with Sophie d'Houdetot, an episode not lacking in ridiculousness.[13]

Julie explains her own situation after the marriage to her "inseparable" cousin:

Misfortune to the one who has no longer anything to desire! He loses, so to speak, all his possessions. One enjoys less what one obtains than what one hopes to obtain, and one is happy only before reaching happiness. In fact, a greedy and limited man, made for desiring all and obtaining little, received from heaven a consoling force which brings near him all that he desires. . . . But all this prestige disappeared in front of the very object; nothing embellishes any longer this object in the eyes of the owner; one does not imagine what one sees; imagination no longer adorns one's possession in the slightest way. Illusion disappears where enjoyment appears. The land of illusion is in this world the only land worthy of inhabitation, and such is the void of human affairs, apart from the Being existing through Himself, there is nothing beautiful except what is not. . . . To live without suffering is not a state of human being, to live in this way means death. The one who can do everything without the help of God would be a miserable creature; he would be devoid of the pleasure to desire, any other privation would be more tolerable.[14]

What is worthy of being desired is not an object but the fact of desiring desire itself. If an object is desirable, that is because desire embellishes it with illusion; desire, in other words, invents—or at least transforms—its object. In this sense, the object becomes the epitome of the material world, whereas desire is elevated to the level of a spiritual world.

Naturally, there are many types of desires. That which can be satisfied by its object is not higher than the created world. On the contrary, it is the mark of "a greedy and limited man." Only the desire that can never be satisfied by any earthly object is able to transcend its subject. In this respect, Abrams appears to be right in interpreting romanticism in terms of the internalizing of a biblical vision and of the humanizing of a religious heritage or, to use his expression, "the naturalization of supernaturalism."[15]

Julie's passion is also love for a void that can never be filled by the love for creatures or the love for this life. As Rousseau explains the nature of her love in one of his footnotes:

What! God will then only have the left-over of creatures? On the contrary, the room creatures occupy in the human heart is so little that it is still empty while one believes to have filled it with creatures. Only an infinite object can fill the heart.[16]

Suffering is an inherent component of love, since the object of love can never match this lofty feeling. Spiritual love exalted to the extreme is equal to love of emptiness. Julie's view of love reminds us of St. Augustine's distinction between the object of enjoyment and the object of use. The things of this world are objects of use—that is, they are to be used to attain the only proper object of enjoyment and the only one deserving love, namely God. This is because creatures are transient, while the Creator is eternal.

Julie's definition differs from St. Augustine's in that, the author of *On the Trinity,* believes that the love of a creature degrades its subject since the soul concentrates itself on something inferior; whereas the love of the Creator transcends the soul, which concentrates itself on the only superior object.[17] For Julie, however, love of creatures is the expression of love for the Creator and vice versa. In any case, union with the Creator is not realizable in this world, given that a face-to-face meeting with God in this life is impossible except in a brief moment of ecstasy.

One may state that spiritual love—or the desire for desire—is comparable with this vision in that enjoyment in this world can result only from illusion, and the real object of desire is inferior to the desire itself. Beauty in this world exists only in negating its creatures—in a kind of nothingness.

Nevertheless, the "land of illusion" is not the divine world but the country of fiction, the country of art, or the country of *Julie, ou la nouvelle Héloïse.* In this land, the lovers live for some impossible passion, which can be found only in the dark recess of memory—like the broken image of God hidden in the human heart.

In this sense, Wolmar's, her husband, attempted therapy of his wife's passion is doomed from the outset, since for the lovers to live means to save their precious memory at any price. As Julie states:

> To live without suffering is not a human existence; to live in this way means death. (French version. 6:8:694)

The art of living is tantamount to the art of desiring, or of loving passionately, desperately, and in memory.

Similarity of Souls

Not only the happiness of the lovers rests in the reconstruction of the past in writing, but also the object of love is the narcissistic image of the self, not the beloved one. Both substitutions can be said to contribute to a "spiritualization" of desire, since either experiential or material existence becomes insignificant. Furthermore, the sublimated desire is a motivation of self-improvement. This self-improvement, however, is not free of social implications.

St. Preux's effort to equal the beloved lady and Julie's need of self-justification both illustrate this point but from two different angles. However, the external inequality of social positions can be overcome only by internal equality in the name of similarity of souls.

The sensitive soul which they share in common not only justifies their love but also places them above the society that condemns it in the name of "social hierarchy." The sensitive soul is the source of love, and love is the proof of the excellence of this soul. At the same time, to love implies suffering—the mark of sensitivity that distinguishes our heroes from the common people. St. Preux writes:

What a fatal gift from Heaven is a sensitive soul! He who receives it must expect to have only pain and sorrow on this earth. The plaything of the air and the seasons, his fate is determined by sunlight or mists, cloudy or clear weather, and he will be content or sad as the winds blow. A victim of prejudices, he will find in society's absurd precepts an invincible obstacle to the just desires of his heart. Men will punish him for having sincere sentiments in every affair and for passing judgment on it according to that which is true rather than that which is conventional. But he alone is enough to create his own misery by indiscreetly giving himself up to the divine allure of the good and the beautiful while the heavy chains of necessity attach him to ignominy. He seeks supreme happiness without remembering that he is only mortal. His heart and his reason are incessantly at war, and his limitless desires prepare eternal privations for him. (1:26:72)

In Laclos's novel, the libertines forever search for their playthings in order to play with their victims' sensitivities. Here, St. Preux also victimizes himself as the plaything of fate. To this extent, both libertinism and preromantic love are sentimental games. The difference is that the former is active, while the latter, passive.

In St. Preux's case, sensitivity is proportional to vulnerability. The greater the sensitivity, the more one suffers, not because the subject is inadequate to the world, but because the world is inadequate to the subject. Suffering is not the price that the individual pays for the original sin but the price an imperfect world exacts from those who differ from it because of their greater perfection. And the higher the price, the more sublime the individual, for the heroes' tragic fate is the very proof of their excellence. In the same vein, their love is doomed, since genuine passion cannot be realized in this imperfect and unauthentic world.

In this case, St. Preux's interpretation of the relationship between the individual and the world is not so different from that of the Marquise de Merteuil. Both justify their nonconformism by the divergence between truth and convention in society. Once again, Laclos's libertines want to take advantage of this divergence by adopting a hypocritical attitude, whereas Rousseau's heroes refuse to go along with conventions in the name of their "lofty love." To this extent, love represents individual ethics that support lovers in their resistance to collective ethics or social conventions—as in the Chinese novel *The Dream of the Red Chamber*.

Nevertheless, suffering—the price that the lovers have pay for their sublimity—at the same time diminishes their perfection. Paradoxically, the superiority of the lovers to the world demands recognition from the world, just as Merteuil's superiority requires the recognition of her partner, Valmont, in *Les Liaisons dangereuses*. Since libertinism is antisocial, the recognition of a single partner suffices to affirm the superiority of a "demoniac" character.

Spiritual love has a more ambiguous position *vis-à-vis* social norms: since the lovers are "angelic," they cannot completely overlook social convention. The lover's admiration for the beloved must be justified—or at least justifiable—by the admiration of the common people.

Merteuil's "fortress of the self" is also the "jail" of the self; since she has to follow her own principles, the possibility of unrestricted pleasure is ruled out. Julie's passion requires virtue greater than the social conventions that limit passion. In both cases, the self-control becomes more impassive than the requirements of social norms which are supposed to mitigate against individual choice. After her marriage, Julie writes to St. Preux about her behavior toward her husband:

> It is not enough for her to be respectable; she must be respected as well. It is not enough for her to do nothing but good; she must moreover do nothing which is not approved. A virtuous woman must not only deserve her husband's esteem but also obtain it. If he blames her, she is to blame, and even were she innocent, she is in the wrong as soon as she is suspected, for even keeping up appearances is part of her duty. (2:18:206)

This attitude of women is very convenient for the male ego. Julie exists only in accordance with the image in the eyes of her husband. Her consciousness is only justifiable by her husband's approval. She is the perfect property of her lord, both physically and mentally. In order to live up to her master's expectations, Julie demands of herself much more than is demanded of an ordinary wife.

She must respect the social order that insists on the renunciation of the passion which unifies her and her lover. "Respectable" (*honnête*) refers to Julie as an active agent—a quality which is insufficient. "Respected" (*honoré*) refers to Julie as a passive object, which depends on the action of an outsider.

Paradoxically, as a passive object, Julie has to be more responsible for herself not only in terms of her own actions, but also in terms of another's behavior toward her. "Honor" and "good" are among the most commonly accepted ethical values that stand in opposition to their "sublime" passion.

Julie turns these restrictions into her own standard according to which she examines each of her actions. Merteuil also respects the strictures of her own rules more than a normal social being respects social convention. In both cases, the heroines rebel against a certain social norm by imitating it in a rigid way.

Julie copes with social convention in the name of the sensitive soul, while Merteuil does so through hypocrisy and self-control.

Antisocial or not, superiority is not self-sufficient since this quality necessarily results from comparison. Each act of comparison involves the judgment of another. One who recognizes the superiority of another thereby assumes some degree of power over the one being judged. Moreover, the one judged as "superior" is in some manner reduced to the level of the judge. In many cases, the act of recognition contributes to abolishing one's superiority—or, at least, to diminishing the distance between the superior and the inferior.

In order to acquire the recognition of the world, the characters in Rousseau's novel must resort, to a certain degree, to hypocrisy—or at least to artificiality, as in the case of Wolmar's, Julie's husband, therapy of passion. Since one has to forget the present existence—"forgetting he is a man" (*sans se souvenir qu'il est homme*)—in order to safeguard one's sensitive soul, the sensitive soul itself becomes fictitious, based on a fiction regarding the human condition in general.

Thus, great sensitivity is not only a mark of superiority but also of weakness, since it can survive in this world only through a fictional identity. As Lacan states in *"Le Stade du miroir,"*

> But the important point is that this form situates the agency of ego, before its social determination, in a fictional direction, which will always remain irreducible for the individual alone, or rather, which will only rejoin the coming-into-being (*le devenir*) of the subject asymptotically, whatever the success of the dialectical syntheses by which he must resolve as *I* his discordance with his own reality.[18]

Like the specular image of the self, the inner world of the lover must manifest itself through some form. Thus formulated through the eyes of others, the subjective world can no longer claim to be self-sufficient; and the sensitive soul is not an independent entity but is, to a large extent, an image defined by social norms.

However much the lovers want to distinguish themselves from the common people, they must nevertheless fulfill certain expectations of their society, which determines their *"devenir."* Only in two contexts can they seemingly preserve the independence of their subjectivity. They can set up a double standard for the society and the individual, and act "discreetly"—as Wolmar, Julie's husband, describes his own action—but passion controlled in this way is no longer a "devouring flame" and loses its sublimeness. Or they can overlook "*I* his discordance with his own reality"—but by denying the human condition, one denies the presumed reality.

Nobility is, to a large extent, turned into madness. Therefore, the lovers cannot enjoy "supreme felicity" peacefully—not even in their narcissistic fictional world because the outside world always interferes with this image. Like the image of God hidden in the human soul, the image of "self" can never reach perfection in this life.

On the one hand, passion can never exist in this world as a totally independent entity because a passionate nature must be dependent on the imperfect world. On the other hand, love is a noble feeling which elevates the lover beyond the imperfect world.

Edouard writes to Claire:

> For the highest reason is only attained through the same power of the soul which gives rise to great passions, and we serve philosophy worthily only with the same ardor that we feel for a mistress. (2:2:163)

By fashioning reason in the likeness of passion, Edouard transforms the latter into the source of all noble feelings—a reflection of the centrality of reason in the Age of Enlightenment. As man is made in the likeness of God, so other human feelings are but mere copies of divine passion. But, at the same time, the original takes on certain characteristics of its copies. Like reason, passion is not a "wild flame"—a destructive conflagration—but a well-contained, constructive flame. Joan DeJean may overstate this in writing the following passage.

> *Julie* is an immense indictment of the novel, an attempt to contain "violent passions," and a condemnation of the novel as love story.[19]

But it is true that, in Rousseau's novel passion, in spite of its spontaneity, must be controlled—and thus—negated in order to have a positive value.

Paradoxically, the only way of fighting against the setbacks of passion is by experiencing it fully and wholeheartedly. Wolmar's excuse for giving up any attempt to fight against his passion is precisely his lack of any great passion.

The most loving creature in the novel, Julie, also has the strongest sense of self-control; even the lovemaking scene is rationally conceived, following a strict strategy. Passion does not lead to fall, but serves as "support." But how can passion remain fully natural and spontaneous within the limits of reason? And how can reason preserve its solid structure without being overwhelmed by its origins in passion? Not the success, but the failure of solving these problems makes the novel all the more interesting.

If passion includes both reason and spontaneity, the feeling that results from it cannot be free from contradiction. The "pleasure of suffering" (*plaisir à suffrir*), to use St. Preux's oxymoron, has a masochistic undertone.

> Yes, my sweet friend, in spite of absence, privations, alarms, in spite of despair itself, the powerful exertion of two hearts toward each other is always attended by a secret pleasure unknown to tranquil souls. It is one of the miracles of love to make us find pleasure in suffering, and we should regard as the worst of misfortunes a state of indifference and oblivion which would take all the feeling of our misery from us. Let us lament our fate, oh Julie! But let us not envy anyone. On the whole, there is perhaps no existence preferable to ours, and like the goddess who derives all her happiness from herself, hearts which glow with a celestial fire find in their own sentiments a kind of pure and delightful pleasure, independent of fortune and of the rest of the universe. (2:16:201)

"Secret pleasure" (*volupté secrette*) that implies a sexual pleasure in fact results from its "absence" and "privations." Despite its erotic implication, this expression indicates an admiration of the self in its delirium—which originates in the denial of sensuality. In this passage, several expressions experience a reversal of values: "pleasure" is equal to "suffering;" and "misfortune" equals "comfort."

Thanks to this reversal, the lovers establish the independence of their inner world. Passion becomes, in this sense, the supreme reason because of its ability to judge the material world situated below itself. At the same time, this world of passion remains necessarily one of "unreason" because of its autonomous self-referentiality.

What is admirable in the world of the lovers is precisely this combination of reason and madness, pleasure and pain, misfortune and happiness. Thanks to its independence, their world is no longer susceptible to the changes of the outside world. Extreme agitations are turned into stability. This adoration of the self is accomplished on the basis of the likeness to the divine image, to a self-sufficiency existing in the heart of the human being.

Nevertheless, this self-sufficiency is necessarily fictional, since the sensitive soul remains the "prey" of the material world at the existential level. Because of the divergence of the subjective and the objective worlds, a sensitive soul can preserve its independence only by accepting the standards of the objective world—at least apparently. In other words, Rousseau's "sensitive souls," like Laclos's libertines, must resort the same means in order to cope with the divergence of truth and appearance existing in society. Both imitate this objective difference by applying a double standard in their subjective world.

This double standard is manifested also in the relationship between St. Preux and Julie as teacher and student. St. Preux seldom mentions his teaching activities. Instead, he seems to take advantage of his position to seduce his student. What he teaches appears to center in their passion—again, as in the case of Abelard and Héloïse,

> love turned our eyes more frequently to itself than it directed them to the study of the texts.[20]

Even a scientific concept is turned into a metaphor for the lovers' spiritual conformity.

In this sense, Julie has no doubt learned her lessons well, as she writes in one of her letters:

> Our souls touch, so to speak at all points, and we feel an entire coherence. (Correct me, my friend, if I am poorly applying your lessons in physics.) Fate may indeed separate us, but not disunite us. We shall henceforward have only mutual pleasures and mutual pains; and like those magnets of which you were telling me that have, it is said, the same movements in different places, we should have the same sensations though we were at the two poles of the earth. (1:11:47)

The French expression *"aimans,"* which indicates a scientific material "magnet" is turned into a sentimental word *"amans,"* which indicates the relationship between the teacher and the student as "lovers." A lesson that is supposedly scientific is sentimentalized in this semantic shifting. Not only do they resemble "magnets" but also they actually *are* "lovers." In this classroom, any material becomes the expression of their mutual feelings.

Julie's expression "touched at all points" implies that their souls are identical. Furthermore, this likeness is not limited to a stable situation. The metaphor of coherence describes the identity of movements of their souls in terms of speed, direction, and cycle. If they cannot be "disunited," this is because one is the living image of the other—or the shadow of the other with a living soul.

In this sense, their love is no different from that of the hero of Rousseau's play *Narcissus*, who is in love with his own picture dressed up as a girl. But, whereas Narcissus is concerned with a concrete image, Julie and St. Preux focus on a spiritual one. If the student playfully uses what she has learned in a physics class to embellish her speech about love, she seems to take the lesson on love by the same teacher more seriously. The relationship between the educator and the educated is replaced by that between the seducer and the seduced. Nevertheless, Julie's assimilation of the seductive lesson abolishes the passive-active relationship, and the differences between teacher and student, between seducer and seduced, fade before their common desire for desiring each other.

If the student has such readiness to accept this theory of her teacher, this is because she seems to have the same impressions as the teacher.

> My heart was yours from the first sight. I believed that I saw on your face the features of the soul which ought to belong to me. It seems to me that my senses were only an organ for noble sentiments; I loved in you, less what I saw there than what I believed that I felt in myself.[21]

Julie tells this story retrospectively after her marriage to Wolmar. Her use of the simple past of the verb *"croire"* is interesting. Does she still believe in this similarity of soul, or is this belief rooted from the beginning in illusion?

Later, after the wedding in the church, she will use the same tense to express her mental state:

> Je crus me sentir renaître; je crus recommencer une autre vie. (13:18:355)

Here, the same verb used in the same tense connects two mental states that have two contradictory objects of belief. In the first situation, she believes that she and her lover were born for each other, and that they are the spiritual portraits of each other. Several pages later, she believes that marriage imposed by her father is her rebirth. Perhaps, when she describes these past feelings, she still believes in both, but with a certain distance provided by time;. perhaps what she did believe has an undertone of illusion while writing to St. Preux retrospectively.

No matter how lofty this "land" may be, it cannot be cut off from reality. Even the notion of narcissism, which tends to seek a self-satisfaction within the confined subjective world of the lovers, can by no means formulate an independent entity. The reason is not difficult to explain: narcissism is an erotic interest on self-image. As reflections or projections, any images can be formulated only in the light of certain consciousness, which is largely determined by the look of others. Thus, the look of the narcissistic subject is, more than anything else, the look of others, since the concern with the self-image is also a reflection of the effect of this image in the eyes of others.

This point can be easily proved by the lovers' behaviors in Rousseau's novel. First of all, as we have already argued, the superiority of the lovers still need to be based at least on certain social conventions, if not necessarily to be recognized by others. Second, St. Preux and Julie admire their reflections in ways that are deeply marked by social hierarchy or social distinctions.

St. Preux, a commoner, must elevate himself to deserve Julie, whereas the latter, who very often considers her love sinful, needs the same kind of elevation from her lover to justify herself. Of course, these ascending and descending movements may be partially explained by the medieval chivalrous tradition in which the divinized lady can often be reached only after her knight proves himself by a series of heroic acts. The analogical relationship between Rousseau's lovers, however, seems much more realistic.

Julie's instructions to St. Preux concerning how he should behave in Paris show clearly that her lover has to compensate for his lower social status by gaining social power. Later on, in her proposition of marriage between her cousin and her "friend," she again notes St. Preux's inferiority to her cousin in terms of birth.

Nevertheless, the lowly St. Preux is loved by a *"demoiselle"*——using an expression of Rousseau himself in his *Confession*—which no doubt bolsters his self-respect.

> Julie forgotten? Should I not rather forget myself? And how could I be alone for a single moment, I who exist only for you? (1:23:66)

Although St. Preux resorts to hyperbole to exalt his passion, a certain truth remains nonetheless. St. Preux lives under Julie's shadow. To a large extent, his life would have been a meaningless and aimless floating without his love for her. At the same time, Julie exists only as his "image." His love for Julie is also his love for himself which experiences a social elevation in this image. To this extent, one may say that St. Preux's passion can also be interpreted as a passion for the improvement of his social status.

When Julie asks for her portrait back through Claire, St. Preux protests:

Let everything conspire to wrench you from my heart. Let them pierce it, let them rend it, let them break this faithful mirror of Julie; her pure image will not cease to be reflected even in the smallest fragment. Nothing is capable of destroying it. (2:14:195)

The image of Julie is, thus, identical to the image of God in the heart of a believer. It is the essence of a "self" that—hidden, protected, and even broken—remains no less indestructible. The soul is no less than the seat of this image or its "faithful mirror" (*fidelle miroir*)—like God, but also like a noble lady in a more banal sense, and, for St. Preux, Julie does not need to do anything but to exist in order to win this worship.

To this extent, the relationship between the two lovers can be considered to be a spiritual version of the relationship between a noble person and a commoner; just occupying a place in the heart of his lover is an act of elevation. Nevertheless, his attempts to rise to the same level as the noble Julie through his actions are doomed, since "doing" cannot replace "being."

At the same time, Julie's portrait seems even more important for St. Preux at this moment. The heart of the man is the image of the woman, whereas the image of the woman is the man's "self." In this endless process of mirroring, both lovers benefit from the other as the image of his or her self. Julie projects an image of a "doer"—which is otherwise unrealistic for a woman; St. Preux enjoys his own nobleness in the love of a noble lady despite his quality of a commoner.

As St. Preux writes in his letter:

If it is difficult to obtain your hand, it is even more so to deserve it, and that is the noble task which love imposes on me. (2:19:211)

Thus, the two identical souls love each other from different positions. While St. Preux considers his love for Julie as an elevation factor in his life, Julie cannot help but feel guilty for loving him. Her sense of guilt presumably stems in part from her devotion, but it is also reinforced by their social difference. Consequently, her need for self-justification is never completely absent from her feelings. Very often, the deeper her sentiments, the more guilty she feels and the more she urges her lover to justify her love.

> I know my fate, I sense the horror of it, and yet one consolation is left me in my despair. It is the only one, but it is sweet. It is from you that I expect it, my dear friend. Since I no longer dare think of myself, I think with more pleasure of the one I love. I give you all the esteem that you have taken from me, and you become only more dear to me by compelling me to despise myself. Love, this fatal love which destroys me, gives you new value; you are elevated while I am degraded, and your soul seems to have profited from all the debasement of mine. Therefore, from now on be my only hope. It is for you to justify my crime, if you can, cover it with the honesty of your sentiments, let your merit efface my shame, and excuse with the strength of your virtues the loss of mine that you occasioned. Be my whole being, now that I am nothing. The only honor I have left is wholly in you, and as long as you are worthy of respect, I shall not be completely contemptible. (1:32:84)

Love debases Julie and elevates her lover, in order to put them on equal footing. She falls because of love. Yet, only through love, can she hope to be saved or, more precisely, through her lover—the cause of her fall—considered as a redeemer. But the fall is inherent in his social status—thus in the present—and the redemption can only exist as a hope and be anticipated in the future—an infinitely distant future.

The task is, in fact, impossible to fulfill, since St. Preux cannot change her awareness of their social differences no matter what he does. To this extent, the potential savior remains forever a sinner. The "consolation" of the beloved is imaginary and turns into reproach addressed to the lover for his inability to fulfill her expectations. In order to justify her love for him, therefore, Julie attributes to St. Preux her own qualities. Her friend is no longer "the other" but a copy of herself: "Glances at myself" become those "at the one I love." (1: 32:84)

Self-esteem becomes esteem for the beloved. St. Preux, however, must somehow objectify within himself this image of his lover, as she says in another letter:

> I should like to add as many virtues as a mad passion has
> made me lose; and being no longer able to respect myself, I
> like to respect myself still in you. (1:44:104)

In this sense, her past "virtues" are the present burdens for
St. Preux who struggles to embody the faded image in order to
justify the self-esteem of his beloved. This justification is possible
only if he can "love perfectly." (1:55:124)

But, on one level, the perfection of love is impossible because of the imperfection of the world which separates the lovers
with its social hierarchy. On another level, however, it can be
realized. If the lovers can emancipate themselves from the criteria of the objective world by mirroring each other in an endless game of mutual respect and self-appreciation, they can attain
this height.

As love becomes the justification of "self," love of the
"other," in the end, becomes love of the "self" because, in the
world of passion, every single quality is interchangeable through
the communion of love. To praise the nobility of the beloved is to
exalt the noble nature of one's own passion which, in turn, justifies one's own existence. After his trip around the world, St.
Preux states in his letter to Claire:

> I have circled the entire globe, and I have not been able to
> escape you for a moment. We may try as we like to flee
> from what is dear to us; its image, quicker than the sea and
> the winds, follows us to the end of the universe, and every-
> where we go we carry there what gives us life. (4:3:281)

Claire and Julie (which means Julie herself, St. Preux uses a
plural object in order to avoid the implication of adultery) are
unique because of St. Preux's heart "which knew how to love
them" (*qui sût les aimer*). Moreover, the unique function of the
two women is "to be able to console" (*puisse consoler*) the same
heart. The two subjunctives are both related to the heart. In other
words, the quality of uniqueness of the two women—or, more
precisely, of Julie herself—is perceived only from the point of
view of the lover.

Her uniqueness exists only in her lover's heart. If her image
gives life to her lover, he, on the other hand, gives life to this

image. Social positions and sexual differences largely determine the rules of the complex mirror-game called spiritual love.

Divinization or Self-Projection?

The divinization—and consequent reification—of the woman is, in a sense, the product of the man's projection. The lover and the husband project their self-images onto Julie's personal feelings freely, and thus largely ignore her emotions hidden behind a veil of mystification. Julie herself, however, reinforces her mystified image by her silence and discretion—important virtues for her sex.

In fact, the divinization of the beloved is not qualitatively different from the admiration of society for the perfectly virtuous noble lady. The sum of esteem that she gets from society is the proof of her divine nature. In other words, her "divinity" is also based on some social conventions. Furthermore, the conventionalization of "divine" passion is not devoid of certain mercantile values.

Julie's "divine" nature results largely from her "gift of loving" (*don d'aimer*) which requires "a countergift" "possession of the beloved" (*contredon*). In this sense, love becomes a matter of exchange. Nevertheless, the exchange does not limit itself to this worldliness. Julie's divinization still largely results from the notion of love as religious faith. In the same vein, Julie's devotion is the expression of her overflowing human love.

As we have seen, narcissism plays an important role in the discourse of love. The divinization of the beloved represents an extension of the self: as she becomes a divine image, so is her lover also elevated to the level of divinity. Julie herself contributes to the divinization of her image to the extent that she often demands of herself something which is humanly impossible. If she does not fulfill her own expectations—which is natural—she will criticize herself as if she had committed an inexcusable crime. Indeed, after each scene of self-criticism, she receives, either from her lover or from her cousin, more copious expressions of admiration.

> Look at my shame, and grieve if you know how to love. My mistake is irreparable; my tears will never dry. Oh you who

caused them to flow, be fearful of attempting to end such just sorrows; my whole hope is for them to be made eternal. The worst of my crimes would be to be comforted for them, and the ultimate disgrace is to lose, along with innocence, the sentiment which makes us love it. (1:32:84)

By overstating her faults, she exaggerates her feelings of "shame" (*honte*), which may substitute "innocence" at the end of this paragraph. In other words, innocence has to be "loved," as does shame and the shameful subject in her deep regret for her perfect innocence. The stronger her shame is, the greater her innocence.

Similarly, by paying for a limited mistake with an infinite amount of guilt, she makes herself not inferior but superior to those who have not committed the same mistake, thanks to the greatness of her regret. As the lovers repeatedly state, the intensity of passion goes together with the greatness of the soul.

By dint of self-reproach over the eternalized "pain," she glorifies shame and distinguishes herself from the common people because of the "innocence" of her soul. In this case, her incorruptible morality is expressed by her sense of guilt. Like love, self-respect is fulfilled also in a negative way in Julie's case.

Claire shows considerable psychological insight into her cousin's self-condemnation. She discusses the guilt which Julie feels at her mother's death in a letter:

If the reproaches that my afflicted cousin makes of herself over her mother's death were well-founded, this cruel memory would, I confess, poison that of your love, and such a distressing idea should forever extinguish it, but do not believe in her grief. It deceives her, or rather, the imaginary cause with which she likes to increase it is only a pretense to justify its excess. Her tender heart is always fearful of not being sufficiently afflicted, and it is a kind of pleasure for her to add to her anguish all that which can sharpen it. She deludes herself, you may be sure; she is not sincere with herself. (3:7:239)

Julie searches for the reason—not to justify herself, but to condemn herself even for "imaginary cause" (*chimérique motif*), because she "likes" (*aime*) to increase her own suffering. Why does Julie need this fiction of "affliction?" Largely because suffering is a "pleasure," a pleasure of refusal.

She says "yes" to the requirements of conventional society by sacrificing her personal needs. But by saying "no" to herself, she subverts the social norms she otherwise so conscientiously respects.

At the same time, this attitude reinforces her image of a perfect social being even further. The masochistic act of self-condemnation is the source of pleasure; as in the act of confession, it purifies the soul of all faults.

To a large extent, self-condemnation is a way of creating new obstacles to the lovers, since the lover considers the beloved as his or her self-image. Self-condemnation contributes to making love impossible. Given the relationship of lover as self, Julie, by condemning herself, also condemns her lover:

> It is perhaps important to your complete recovery that I tell you all that remains in my heart. Monsieur de Wolmar is older than I. If in order to punish me for my faults Heaven would deprive me of the worthy husband whom I so little deserve, my firm resolution is never to take another. If he has not had the good fortune to find a chaste girl, he at least will leave behind a chaste widow. You know me too well to believe that having made this declaration to you I may ever retract it. (3:20:262)

Julie herself passes sentence to her passion for St. Preux: their love is not consumable in this world because of its past. In fact, a past that Julie considers so sinful and earthly allows Julie to create a pure and heavenly present by negating any possible physical pleasure for herself—even in the most legitimate situation. Instead of social law, she is following divine law—the law of her "divine" consciousness which is, by far, more uncompromising than society.

On the day of her wedding, she seems to sacrifice forever her love for St. Preux in the church through "a kind of emotion (she) had never experienced." The nature of this emotion is "terror" and "fright," which means passion, although in a negative sense.

Before this moment, she had passively accepted the marriage under pressure from her father. From now on, she will participate body and soul in this marriage. Religious passion and awe of God, reinforced by social authority in the name of her father, succeeds in negating, for the time being, her personal passion and her love for St. Preux.

Julie's life has been torn by these two passions: the passion of restriction and the passion of expansion. These two apparently contradictory passions are in reality complementary. On the one hand, without the restriction of her faith, her love could not be everlasting. On the other hand, because of her love and her guilt, she has an additional need for religion in order to provide support or balance in her life. Therefore, in spite of apparent contradictions, Julie's love is proportional to her faith, so that, at the end of the work and in the long speech before her death, she unites religious faith with human love.

This ability to unite what is apparently irreconcilable is the source of Julie's uniqueness. As St. Preux exclaims:

> What woman ever joined tenderness to virtue as you do, and tempering one with the other, made both more charming? (1:10:45)

"Tenderness" or private life, and "virtue" or the social standard of public life, are two sides of a problem that always preoccupied the author of *Julie, ou la Nouvelle Héloïse* in both his fictional and his political writings. To what extent is it possible to merge these antagonistic qualities?

By ascribing success to Julie, Rousseau seems to conclude that the possibility is limited. Julie is ever the skillful acrobat trying to balance the two sides, but she reaches the stage of perfection only with her death which forever stabilizes the image of her subjective world. But the truth, interred with the dead body, therefore remains eternally unfathomable. St. Preux calls this harmony "divine accord:"

> It is from you that one must learn all the goodness, all the probity possible in a human soul, and, most of all, that divine union of virtue, love, and nature, which never existed

except in you! No, there is no virtuous affection which does not have its place in your heart, which is not distinguished there by your particular sensibility. And for the better regulation of my own, just as I have often deferred all my actions to your will, I am convinced that all my sentiments must also be determined by yours. (1:21:61)

The three qualities of virtue, love, and nature belong to three different realms: the social, personal, and universal. Their agreement can exist only on the level of the divine, in that it consists of an independent world that does not need any "complément."

But this "divine accord" is humanly impossible because the three different codes are not mutually dependent. Since they may very well move in different directions, any harmony is necessarily momentary. This "accord" could last only if Julie's heart were motionless. But her heart is distinguished precisely by its "sensitivity," the source of emotions and of motions. Its dynamic quality is too human not to threaten this "divine accord." And each movement inevitably threatens to shatter the harmony of the previous moment.

This stable image of harmony is largely St. Preux's creation. Because he claims that his actions and feelings depend on Julie's will and sentiment, this divine world is also his idealized self-image as well as a metaphor for their passion.

Rousseau makes an interesting remark in one of his footnotes following Wolmar's statement that St. Preux is in love with the image of Julie which he had seen in the past, not with the present Julie.

You are quite foolish, you women, who would like to give constancy to a sentiment as fickle and transient as love. Everything changes in nature, everything is in a continual flowing, and you want to inspire constant passion? By what right do you claim to be loved today because you were yesterday? Keep thus the same face, the same age, the same mood; be always the same, then one will always love you if one can. But to change ceaselessly and to hope that one always loves is tantamount to hoping that at each moment, one ceases to love you. This is not to look for constant hearts, but to look for the hearts as changeable as yourselves.[22]

Following this logic, constant love becomes impossible due to the changeability of human nature. The constancy of love can exist either on the basis of illusion—the lover sees what does not exist in the beloved—or in memory—the lover deliberately remains blind to the changes that have occurred in the beloved. In both cases, passion is determined by the lover's subjective choice to remain the dupe and has almost nothing to do with the objective reality of the beloved.

In other words, passion can endure only if the object of love plays a far less important role than the subject of love, because love depends on the image of the beloved which is created by the lover. Therefore, love necessarily carries a narcissistic undertone. As in the case of Julie's "divine accord," we can assume that this situation is based on the illusion and the memory of the subject, an image recreated in St. Preux's imagination.

However, the harmony within Julie's heart is precious not because it is divine or indestructible, but because it is human and fragile. St. Preux sometimes misunderstands its nature, neglecting the fragility hidden behind the apparent calm.

> What prodigy of Heaven are you then, inconceivable Julie? And by what art, known to you alone, can you assemble so many incompatible impulses in one heart? (1:31:81)

These two questions can be considered rhetorical exclamations over Julie's superior nature. But they may also be taken in a more literal sense, as expressions of St. Preux's bewilderment at this nature which seems "inconceivable" and "incompatible."

As difficult as Julie's personality appears for him to grasp, St. Preux, nevertheless, does not need to understand her in a complete sense. On the contrary, he needs a certain margin of incomprehensibility to mystify and divinize the beloved for his own sake.

By emphasizing her uniqueness, as in "you alone," St. Preux refuses to understand her as a person capable of any uncontrollable emotions. Her subjective world is perfectly under control. What is left for him to do is to admire his own image in this divine image, thanks to his peaceful love for the perfect lady.

Wolmar, who claims to be a most understanding person, cannot avoid being tempted by this mystification, as he writes to Claire:

> A veil of wisdom and propriety puts so many folds around her heart, that it is no longer possible for the human eye to penetrate to it, not even her own.[23]

This veil is indispensable for both lover and the husband to allow themselves to project their own wishful thinking more freely. In other words, St. Preux can justify his existence in loving a woman who personifies perfection, whereas Wolmar may admire himself in his artfulness in saving his loving wife from the disturbing memory of her past passion. In this sense, the divinization of the woman is another version of her objectification—woman as an object of free projection.

St. Preux says in his letter:

> I find you too perfect for a mere mortal. I should believe you to be a purer species, if this devouring fire which pierces my being did not unite me to yours and did not make me feel that they are one and the same. No, no one in the world knows you. You do not know yourself. My heart alone knows you, feels you, knows what place you are to occupy in it. My Julie! Ah, if you were only adored, what homage would be robbed from you! Ah! If you were only an angel, how much of your value would you lose! (1:38:97)

Without St. Preux's knowledge, Julie cannot appreciate her own excellence. The one who is capable of knowing the other's perfection is superior to the object of his knowledge, because this requires not only a degree of similarity and affinity but also a broader vision that includes the object itself.

Moreover, the subject of knowledge actively assigns a place to the object who passively accepts it. Only through her lover may Julie become conscious of herself; that is, through his worship of Julie, St. Preux is able to "put" Julie "in her place," and, by his superior knowledge, to save her from self-ignorance.

However subjective this value judgment may be, Julie's perfection has at least two seemingly objective bases: her recognition of others and her loving nature. One can also say that these two bases are two sides of the same coin. As Claire explains to Julie:

> That friends, acquaintances, servants, neighbors, and the entire village may adore you unanimously and take the most tender interest in you—all that, my dear, is a less likely coincidence which would not have occurred if there were not in your person some particular reason. Do you know what this reason is? It is neither your beauty, nor your wit, nor you grace, nor anything of all that known as the talent of pleasing. It is, rather, that tender heart and that sweetness of affection which is matchless; it is the talent of loving, my child, which makes you loved. On can resist everything except benevolence, and there is no surer means of acquiring the affection of others than by giving them your own. A thousand women are more beautiful than you; several have as many graces. Only you have, along with these graces, an indefinable more seductive quality which not only pleases but affects and ravishes every heart. One feels that your heart asks only to give itself, and the delightful sentiment which it is looking for comes in turn to look for it. (2:5:172)

Love is a "gift." As Benveniste explains in his "Lexicon and culture," etymologically speaking, "to give" *donner* also "to take" *prendre*.

> The freedom of gift obliges the receiver to give a "countergift." This leads to a coming and going of gifts offered or given in return.[24]

To love is to possess or to exact the return of a sentimental gift. By loving others, Julie possesses their love, because love is more "seductive" (*séduisant*) than any other qualities.

But loved by them, she must also pay the price. Here, Julie faces a dilemma. She consults her cousin as to whether she should accept Edouard's, the passionate English Lord, offer: that is to live with St. Preux in Edouard's domain for the rest of her life. While reminding Julie of how much she is loved by everyone in her family—especially by her "inséparable" cousin herself—Claire seems to demand the *contredon* of love—namely, duty—in order to force her to give up her passion for St. Preux. At this moment, Julie is torn between her love for St. Preux and for her family, and Claire adds to the family side a new weight which changes the balance of Julie's affection.

Looked at from this angle, Julie's personality is not so mysterious. Claire explains to Julie:

> One feels that your heart asks only to give itself, and the delightful sentiment which it is looking for comes in turn to look for it. (2:5:172)

Before her death, Julie still wishes to keep an eye on her beloved family and friends, and to gather around her tomb all those whom she cherishes. Indeed, even after her death, her lover and her cousin—as well as her husband—remain possessed by her love, each embraced by the past shared with this loving soul.

To this extent, she is a good "sister" of Merteuil—with an important difference. Whereas Julie possesses others by tenderness and through the power of love, the Marquise does so by the absence of love and through the power of machination.

Which method is more efficient? Perhaps one can say that Julie's psychological impact on others is more durable, although less dazzling. But both give up something in the exchange. Merteuil pays a price for her domination, that of self-control; and Julie's possession of love is also marked by an exchange of obligations and duties. "The talent of loving" is no doubt superior to "the talent of pleasing," because "there is no surer means of acquiring the affection of others than by giving them your own."

As Claire states in short, the core of this relationship is not that of lover-beloved but of giver-receiver. What is at stake is more a two-way act of give-and-take rather than a mysterious ascent toward heaven, since the action of giving is simultaneously the action of receiving. Love as a "gift" is, first of all, a gift of obligation.

Moreover, this gift of loving and being loved puts Julie almost on a plane equal to that of God. As St. Preux exclaims:

Tell me, who then is this unique mortal whose least influence is in her beauty, and who, like the eternal powers, makes herself equally adored both through the good and through the evil she does? Alas! She has robbed me of everything, the cruel woman, and I love her more for it. The more miserable she makes me, the more I find her perfect. It seems that all the torment she causes me is a new instance of her merit for me. (2:10:187)

Love is not only a medium of exchange but also a power—the utmost power that a human being can dream of possessing. This power aims at making the lovers "equally adored both through the good and through the evil she does," as St. Preux writes. The relationship between Julie and those whom she loves becomes that which exists between creator and creatures, since her unlimited affection enables others to experience a new kind of spiritual life and love with her.

Her system is totalizing: as she creates them in her own likeness, they are "forced" to love her. Like God, she personifies love. Claire says further:

No one can see you or think of you coolly. (4:9:299)

Julie's kingdom is limitless and reaches out without distinction to affect all kinds of human beings, regardless of their genders and social positions.

One would say that, nothing on earth being equal to the need to love with which she is devoured, her excess of sensibility is forced to ascend to its source. Hers is not a loving heart like Saint Theresa's, which deceives itself and will mistake its object. Hers is a truly inexhaustible heart which neither love nor friendship could consume and which carries its superabundant affections to the only Being worthy of accepting them. Love of God does not detach her from His creatures; it does not make her severe or sharp. All her attachment, proceeding from the same cause, one being enlivened by the other, become more charming and sweet, and for my part, I think she would be less devout if she loved her father, her husband, her children, her cousin, and myself less tenderly. (5:5:349)

Julie's devotion results from the overflowing of love. In the case of Saint Theresa,[25] sensual love is a metaphor for faith. While in Rousseau's novel, in contrast, faith is turned into a metaphor for human love—not only because Julie's devotion comes from too much "love" and "friendship," but also because "love of God" is reduced to an expression of human love.

As a result, the relationship between creator and creature forms a chiasma with the relationship between signifier and signified—the creator becomes the signifier of its creatures. In the end, both remain signifiers of the "same cause": Julie's loving nature.

As St. Preux's idol, Julie must be the mirror image of his inner world. But the mirror image would have lost its *raison d'être* if it did not contribute to an escape from the present condition that limits the inner world. To this extent, the mirror image represents otherness, the opening toward another world, or a fixed point to which the reflected self can refer. By divinizing Julie's loving nature and making it the point of reference of love for both creator and created, St. Preux seems to legitimize to a large extent his self as centered on the reflection of Julie's divine nature.

Carl Schmitt defines romanticism as "subjectified occasionalism."[26] In his opinion, a certain Western metaphysical tradition portrays God as the ultimate authority, for whom the whole world is merely an "occasion." By replacing God with the self, the romantic reduces the world to an occasion to exercise his or her own fantasy.

As far as religion is concerned, there exists at least an external and objective criterion; whereas romanticism is utterly free, so to speak, of any responsibility in a realistic sense. The ethical distinctions between truth and falsehood, good and evil, blur before the aesthetic concerns of an indifferent contemplator. To a large extent, the so-called spiritual love results from such an aestheticization of certain social norms.

Schmitt considers the author of *Julie, ou la Nouvelle Héloïse* an important figure of romanticism. The analysis of Rousseau's novel may confirm this point in that the author treats passion essentially from an aesthetic point of view.

He exalts and elevates the value of "a sensitive soul" with passion, illusory as it is, being the supreme value over reason, reality, and social law. More precisely, passion is the loftiest of all feelings because it is based on illusion. The illusory nature of passion allows a passionate lover to establish a self-referential world.

Furthermore, since the real world is imperfect, perfect beauty resides in nothingness—in illusion. This attitude frees the preromantic seer or the aesthete from any responsibility toward society or toward the "real" world. He or she can play with reality to satisfy his or her fantasy (or passion) or to nourish his or her illusion. In this case, social values such as truth and morality take on significance only insofar as they are aesthetic elements in the subjective world of a "sensitive soul."

The interesting question, however, is not whether these descriptions fit Rousseau's novel, but whether they are characteristics of romanticism in particular. Thus defined, romanticism becomes a special kind of individualism that transforms the objective world into a metaphor for a self-referential world in the name of art.

Nevertheless, the same thing can be roughly said of *The Dream of the Red Chamber*, the eighteenth-century Chinese novel studied in the last chapter of this book. In fact, passion is a perfect object to express this "aesthetic version of individualism" as the counterpart of the restrictions imposed by reality. To this extent, the difference between the two ways of portraying idealized passion is one of form more than of content.

Ernst Block used a metaphor to describe yet another form of individualism—nihilism.

When one has a tooth out, there is a hole. Following the shape of the tooth, the hole has this or that form. Therefore, nihilism or atheism takes various forms according to how it occurs in India or in China, in a Catholic, a Protestant, or a Moslem country. Because what has disappeared was different, it had a different figure. Consequently, nihilism is first of all a residual phenomenon, its role is to offer consolation for the loss of something positive. As a result, it takes a large number of forms that cannot be compared one with another. They have only one thing in common: nihil, nothingness.[27]

To a degree, passion is also a "residual phenomenon." We must, therefore, study the "positive" opponents, such as ethics or religion, if we are to compare its different forms. As we have seen, the lovers in Rousseau's novel choose writing as a main method of spiritualizing physical love, while the lovers in Ts'ao Hsüeh-ch'in's novel express their mutual feelings mainly in a negative fashion. We cannot simply explain this difference only in terms of their individual genius, but rather in terms of their social, ideological, and cultural makeup.

Even though the configuration of the hole is not necessarily similar to that of the lost tooth, we can always find some traces of the past in this hole of "nothingness." Passion illustrates the "lost tooth" especially because this "residual phenomenon" can be taken largely as an aesthetic version of social norms.

4

Passion without Words

In Rousseau's preromantic novel *Julie, ou la Nouvelle Héloïse*, the lovers are distinguished from common people by their "sensitive soul." In Ts'ao Hsüeh-ch'in's[1] *The Dream of the Red Chamber*,[2] the lovers are characterized by their "sublime essence" (*ling-hsing*) or (*ling-ch'i*.)[a] Both the French and the Chinese terms describe an individual quality suggestive of a vocation for passionate existence or, at least, for an existence beyond the practical concerns of everyday life.

In both novels, love is, to a large degree, desexualized or sublimated; but the process of sublimation remains very different in each of the works. As discussed in the third chapter of this book, by replacing the physical object of desire, the narration of passion—enriched by a long rhetorical tradition of love that distinguishes the spiritual from the physical following the example of religious faith—functions in Rousseau's novel as the major means of sublimation.

In the Chinese novel, the situation is more complicated. Writing in the absence of a similar discursive tradition, Ts'ao

Hsüeh-ch'in must "invent" a rhetoric that can function as an instrument of desexualization based on the language of sensual love in general. Whereas in the Christian tradition language is supposed to serve as one of the last stages in the representation of the ultimate truth, in the Confucian context, its primary connection is with constitutional law or social conventions.

As a Confucianist thinker, Hsün-tzu states:

> Kings are the ones who defined names, the names of criminal law came from the Shang Dynasty, the names of titles started with the Chou dynasty, the names of ritual ceremonies resulted from the Chou *Book of Ritual*.[3]

In this sense, *The Dream of the Red Chamber* subverts conventional society not only by placing the code of individual passion over collective ethics, but also by its urge to reinvent a language of love, which may more efficiently communicate and distinguish the lovers' mutual feelings from common lust. Even though the lovers, however, seem to communicate their passion mostly in a negative fashion—namely, through quarrels—the connotations of certain words that refer to their axiological system transgress the traditional relationship between "name and substance" (*ming shih*)[b] which serves as the basis of Confucian society. In Chinese language, "name" (*ming*) also means language. Confucian "rectification of names" signifies the adjustment of the relationship between a linguistic sign and its referential meaning, which may be merely subjective. So I will refer to names as linguistic signs or as words since, in plain language, *ming* is also a word or, more precisely, a "common name of a thing or a matter."

Because "the rectification of names"[4] (*cheng-ming*) is an important concept of Confucian morality, the relationship between "name" and "substance" is largely ethicized. To this extent, overlooking linguistic conventions constitutes an important step toward freedom from social obligations.

The author of *The Dream of the Red Chamber* has recourse to the Taoist tradition, especially to the ideas of Chuang-tzu, which are very often sensualized in the novel.[5] According to Chuang-tzu, language does not deserve too much consideration, since its major function is that of differentiation. All differentiations can only be artificial and arbitrary, because nature itself is an undifferentiated totality. Even the distinctions between reality and illusion, and between life and dream, collapse: each of those terms can be transformed into the other.

Chuang-tzu claims to use an "absurd language" (*huang-t'ang yen*)[c] that does not differentiate things in a judgmental mode. *The Dream of the Red Chamber* uses the same kind of language—"absurd language"—which breaks the conventional meanings of certain linguistic signs.

For example, "obscene" (*yin*)[Int.p] traditionally has only pejorative denotations, but the author uses this term as a substitute for the term "sentiment" (*ch'ing*)[Int.o] to describe the most important characteristic of the adolescent hero, Chia Pao-yü. Does this mean that the author of *The Dream of the Red Chamber* condemns the concept of passion with the judgmental expression "obscene"? Or does it mean that, by this choice, he voices his contempt for the moral code implied in the same expression? The second possiblity seems the more plausible, since *The Dream of the Red Chamber* is characterized by its openendedness in conflicting codes.

The fairy Disenchantment, the author's key spokeswoman, states, "To enjoy sensuality is lust, to understand passion is even more lustful."(1:5:146) But precisely *because* of his lust, the hero wins the favor of the fairy Disenchantment, as she herself says in Pao-yü's dream.

This unstable relationship between "name" and "substance" corresponds to the blurred distinction between fiction and life. In fact, the story of *The Dream of the Red Chamber* is situated within several layers of dream. Fiction, dream, and reality are so intertwined that it is very difficult, if not impossible, to distinguish one from another. In this way, the author keeps a safe distance from the threat of the actual world of politics and, to a degree, frees himself from the restrictions of common language as well as the restrictions of social convention.

The author's individualistic use of language helps create the complex personality of the hero. For example, the expressions that the "common people" (*su-jen*)[d] use to criticize his strange behavior are very often turned into descriptions of his "sublime essence," which is beyond the understanding of his judges. In other words, there are at least two levels of language in the novel: one functions within the "Garden of Great View"[6] (*Ta-kuan yüan*)[e] which the hero takes as the embodiment of his inner world; the other is the commonly accepted language that reflects social reality. The same expressions can be interpreted in different—if not opposite—ways, depending on the points of view of the speaker and listener.

Even within the same system of language—as between Pao-yü and Tai-yü—the task of communication is not that easy. Passion requires a process of desexualization in order to become sublime. As in the case of letter-writing for the two lovers in Rousseau's novel, something has to replace the object of physical desire, which is the body.

In China, there was no rhetoric of love relatively free of sensual implications comparable to the one existing during the same period in France. Moreover, the idealization of individual love in contrast to conventional society cannot be devoid of conventions, since the more "admirable" the individual image is, the more the individual has to purify himself or herself of the elements condemned by conventional morality. If not, he or she no longer has enough "admirers" to be "admirable."

As in the case of Rousseau's *Julie, ou la Nouvelle Héloïse*, the sublimation of the transgressive act leads to the same ending arbitrarily prescribed by Julie's father. Moreover, passion in Confucian China has less chance to be mystified and glorified than it does in the West, because Confucianism is mainly an ethical code based on moderation centered on family values.

Naturally, there are always exceptions, such as some poems in *The Book of Songs*, Ch'ü Yüan's *Li sao*, and in *Yüeh-fu* poetry. Later on, love is an important subject in T'ang *Ch'uan-ch'i*, some *tz'u* in the South Sung, and in dramas, of which T'ang Hsien-tsu provides a good example. But the point is that there is no well-defined positive language that identifies sensual love with spiritual love or with religious faith.

The two lovers—especially Pao-yü's female cousin Lin Tai-yü—to a large extent internalize the social conventions that censure passion despite their contempt for the same conventions. To this extent, the exaltation of their passion must even more urgently be desexualized. But, again, the appropriate language is lacking.

Like the author himself, who has to "invent" a language to explain the notion of "passion," the two lovers in the novel must gradually create their own means of communication, either through a suggestive language, poetry, or even the failure of communication, as in quarrels. Neither the author nor the characters seem very successful in this respect, but it is the failure of communication that makes the experience of passion in this novel all the more interesting.

Dream within Dream

The reader of *The Dream of the Red Chamber* is usually struck by the ludicrousness of the novel's supernatural framework. Lucien Miller writes that the supernatural agents seem satirical, amoral, and playful in this novel.[7] Furthermore, intertwined with the fuzzy distinction between the natural and supernatural world, dreams within *The Dream* transform the realistic world into a dream and equate life with illusion.

At the same time, since tears serve as the ink with which the novelist experiences passion in writing his tragic work, illusion is turned into truth through an artistic creation. The divine world represents fictionality within the fiction by confusing the distinction between reality and dream and between existence and nothingness.

The Dream of the Red Chamber is also called *The Story of the Stone*. The magic jade that the hero carries in his mouth when he is born represents, not only the essence of his life, but also the voice of the narrator under the name of "Brother Stone" (*Shih-hsiung*).[f] At the same time, it is on the body of the stone that the text of the novel is inscribed.

In short, the stone is an autobiographical link as well as a tie between the empirical world and textuality. As the narrator states in the first sentence of the novel in the eighty-chapter edition:

The author says himself, after experiencing some dreams and illusions, that he dissimulates the truth and uses the version of the magic jade to write this novel called *The Story of the Stone*.[8]

The stone becomes an "antisign" that hinders the presence from presenting itself through the mark. In the same vein, the use of the third person in the place of the author contributes further to this ambiguity. There is also a series of narrators: the one who introduces the author; the one who uses the first person; the spiritual stone which represents both the author and the text; the Taoist monk Vanitas (*K'ung k'ung tao-jen*)[8] who reluctantly agrees to bring the inscription on the stone into the human world; and Ts'ao Hsüeh-ch'in who edits it after reading and correcting it over ten years.

Between the "I" of the author and the editor called Ts'ao Hsüeh-ch'in, there seems no direct connection at all. But it turns out that he is, in fact, the author. In this case, even the intention of lying is not real, and the camouflage serves only to reveal the identity. What is dissimulated here is the very act of representation.

On the one hand, the stone functions as the representational object par excellence: it does triple duty as author, hero, and text. On the other hand, it does not represent reality but "dissimulates" it unsuccessfully or playfully.

This is not only a clever language game, but also a historical necessity. Ts'ao wrote his novel at a time of political upheaval in China.

After the death of Emperor K'ang-hsi, the new Emperor Yung-cheng dominated the country with terror. The fourth of K'ang-hsi's dozens of sons, Yung-cheng, felt threatened by his brothers. He considered his father's former officials as the potential supporters of his brothers and banished them from the political scene. Because Ts'ao Hsüeh-chin's grandfather was a high official of the late emperor, his family suffered a great deal from this political upheaval.

At the same time, the new emperor mistrusted intellectuals, and kept them quiet by threatening them with the "inquisitions of letters." Writers risked imprisonment if they were not extremely cautious in what they wrote.

For both personal and professional reasons, Ts'ao Hsüeh-ch'in distanced himself as much as possible from the actual world of politics. This necessity, however, coincided with a personal inclination because Ts'ao Hsüeh-ch'in chose to write in a style that created a gap between the fictional language of the novel and language commonly used as a reliable means of communication in society, a style that violates the conventional relationship between the name and its substance, which, in the Confucian tradition, is considered to be the very basis of social law.[9]

In order better to understand this transgressive nature of the stone, we must look closely at its origins as described at the beginning of the novel.

> Long ago, when the goddess Nü-wa was repairing the sky, she melted down a great quantity of rock and, on the Incredible Crags of the Great Fable Mountains, molded the amalgam into 36,501 large building blocks, each measuring 72 feet by 144 feet square. She used 36,500 of these blocks in the course of her building operations, leaving a single odd block unused, which lay, all on its own, at the foot of Greensickness Peak in the aforementioned mountains. (1:1:47)

Both names of the location, "Great Fable" (or "Absurdity") (*Ta-huang*)[h] and "Incredible" (*wu-chi*),[i] describe the essence of the hero which is embodied in the stone, as well as in the nature of the novel, with the stone representing the voice of the narrator. The absurd nature of the hero and the work has been repeatedly emphasized in the novel through this supernatural framework.

In Chapter 7, when Pao-ch'ai looks at the jade, the author writes a poem with the following couplet:

> Nü-wa's stone-smelting is already absurd,
> From this absurdity originates a greater fable. (1:7:54)

Why does the author repeatedly insist on the absurdity of his story? Is he really warning the reader not to take his novel seriously? I would suggest not.

As in the case of *The Mirror for the Romantic*, sometimes one should not look at the "face" of an expression—meaning its ordinary sense—but at its "back." That is, one should try to understand the refracted meaning. *The Mirror for the Romantic* or *The Mirror of Wind and Moon (Feng-yüeh pao-chien)* is among the titles attributed to the novel in the first chapter of *The Dream of the Red Chamber*. The story is about a minor character in the novel, Chia Jui, the son of Pao-yü's teacher. The Taoist monk brings the magic mirror to Chia Jui, who is sick with longing for an unreachable woman, Wang Hsi-feng. The Taoist immortal tells the patient that the mirror can cure his sickness, provided that he looks only at the back of the mirror. But when the young man follows the Taoist's prescription, he sees a frightening skeleton. As the mirror falls, he sees his beloved on the face of mirror. Even though the Taoist has forbidden him to look at the face, he cannot help contemplating the image of the woman and making love with her in a dreamlike state until he dies from complete exhaustion (1:12:251–53). In other words, one cannot understand Ts'ao's work simply through face-values of conventional language. Instead, one needs occasionally to read on the back of commonly accepted meanings of words, such as in the case of "absurd" *huang t'ang*.

The following verses no doubt provide us with a clue for the expression "absurd":

> Pages full of absurd words,
> Penned with hot and bitter tears;
> All men call the author fool,
> Who can really taste the flavor of the book?
> (None his secret message hears). (1:1:51)

If the book appears absurd, it is not because it is nonsensical in itself but because the absurd world cannot discern its "secret message." The apparent absurdity represents an unfathomable depth. Like his stone, the hero's "stupidity" (*ch'ih*)[j] in the eyes of common people dissimulates the "spiritual essence" (*ling-hsing*)[a] which is beyond their comprehension.

The second characteristic of the passage about the origin of the stone is no doubt its uniqueness. Thirty-six thousand five hundred days equals one hundred years or a century. The totality of other stones highlights the singularity of the stone that is left unused. If other stones that repaired the sky form a perfect collectivity, the one left over represents individuality. Throughout the book, the author emphasizes time and again the quality of uniqueness. For example, this couplet describes Pao-yü in the third chapter.

> For uselessness the world's price he might bear;
> His gracelessness in history has no peer. (1:3:102)

The majority of blocks, then, are used in a collective mission that carries a strong moral undertone, that of repairing Heaven. In traditional China, Heaven is a metaphor for the empire, since the emperor is called "the son of Heaven" (*t'ien-tzu*).[k] The individual wanders aimlessly in an amoral world that is characterized by its uselessness.

But is it praiseworthy or blameworthy to be useless? A statement made by Chuang-tzu and partially quoted by the hero offers an answer.

> The trees in the mountains plunder themselves. The grease in the flame sizzles itself. Cinnamon has a taste, so they hack it down, lacquer has a use, so they strip it off. All men know the uses of the useful, but no one knows the uses of the useless.[10]

Usefulness is self-destructive, whereas uselessness is self-protective. In the end, and from the individual's point of view, uselessness is more useful than usefulness. But in Chuang-tzu's text, the usage the author had in mind is how to preserve oneself in the middle of political upheavals, while Ts'ao Hsüeh-ch'in truly desired to use his talent to write his novel. Thanks to its uselessness in the collective and moral mission of repairing Heaven, the unused stone is able to accomplish its individual and amoral purpose of writing the novel.

Usefulness is connected with "truthful" language, as in the case of a book on governing (1:1:50) which pretends to have a serious moral mission, whereas uselessness corresponds to "absurd" language which is aimless.

Again, as in Chuang-tzu's writings, one is ethical while the other is aesthetic. But this aestheticization in *The Dream of the Red Chamber* differs from that of the Taoist philosopher in that it must be sensualized as in most cases in the novel. This individual usage—that is useless according to a social standard—is rooted primarily in sentiment, since "Greensickness" (*ch'ing-keng*)[l] denotes, by a pun, "the sentimental root" (*ch'ing-ken*).[m]

Another fable in the first chapter further elaborates the concept of "passion" (*ch'ing*). The story is narrated by the immortal in Chen Shih-yin's dream.

> On the banks of the Magic River, by the Rock of the Rebirth, there is a Crimson Pearl Herb. The Servant of Divine Stone watered her every day with sweet dew, thereby conferring on her the gift of life. Later on, the Crimson Pearl was nourished with the substance of the purest cosmic essence. Thanks to the vitalized rain and dew, she was able to shed her vegetable shape but only assume the form of a girl. She wandered about outside of the Realm of Separation, eating the Secret Passion Fruit when she was hungry and drinking from the Pool of Sadness when she was thirsty. The consciousness that she owed the stone something for his kindness in watering her began to prey on her mind and ended up by becoming an obsession. At this moment, The Divine Luminescent Stone in Waiting fancied the Red Dust.[11] He would like to take advantage of this peaceful and prosperous period to descend to the world and to experience the illusory fate. He has registered with the office of the fairy Disenchantment. In this case, Disenchantment also inquired about the debt of watering. The fairy girl answered: "I don't have sweet dew here that I can repay him with. The only way in which I could perhaps repay him would be with the tears shed during the whole of a mortal lifetime if he and I were ever to be reborn as humans in the world below." (1:1:53)

After passing through the hands of several copyists, the text inscribed on the stone finally presents itself to the reader. In the inscriptions, we see an anecdote about a man whose name, "Chen Shih-yin," is precisely a pun on "hiding truth" (*chen shih yin*).[n]

Then, in Shih-yin's dream a Buddhist monk tells a Taoist about "an event so weird that it has never been heard of not for a thousand centuries." This series of frameworks functions to reduce to a minimum the referentiality of the tale and, at the same time, to increase to the maximum its playfulness.

At the most superficial level of language, all the characters in this tale are endowed with strange names that indicate an immortal nature. But the names are more ironic or ludicrous than transcendental for these immortals seem to share the earthly values of the human world.

Even the dew with which the stone waters the plant has to be paid back. The fairy Disenchantment here plays the role of an earthly bureaucrat who is concerned with the justice of economic law in her "court" (*an*).[o] Moreover, without any serious theological implications, the whole immortal universe seems to be composed by "chance" (*ou*)[p]—to use the author's very word. The only thing that gives this random structure a certain coherence is the concept of "love" (*ch'ing*) at a symbolic level.

Starting with "root of sentiment" (*ch'ing-ken*), the series of allegedly divine names points to the concept of "love" (ch'ing). "The Rock of three lives" (*san-sheng shih*)[q] indicates the passion between two human beings during different lives. "The fruit of intimate love" (*mi-ch'ing kuo*)[r] is a pun on close relationships and love. The sweet dew with which the stone waters the plant is going to be transformed into tears which are, in this novel, expressions of sentiment.

Furthermore, the Crimson Pearl is the very metamorphosis of tears. Her name is a metaphor for bloody teardrops, and her life comes from sweet dew which she must repay back with tears in the human world. This image again corresponds to the stone's experience under Greensickness Peak when "it passed its days in sorrow and lamentation." In its divine existence, the stone spends all his time shedding tears, just as in its human life, the plant repeats the same experience. They become mirror images of each other.

Their tears are not shed "in vain," however, since they are also the ink with which the author writes this novel.

> Pages full of idle words,
> Penned with hot and bitter tears; (1:1:51)

Like the life of the Crimson Pearl, the "idle (absurd) words" (*huang-t'ang yen*) of the novel are composed of "hot and bitter tears" (*hsin-suan lei*).[s] Words and tears, then are identical. The fantastic and illusory framework is designed to uncover this sorrowful reality through a process of dissimulation.

The author's playfulness toward referential language results from his seriousness toward the concept passion. The tears of which the novel is made transform its absurdity into a reality more real than the actual world since literary creation is, not only the imitation of a tragedy in life, but also tragedy in its own right. Its source is not only artistic inspiration but mainly the tears of everyday life, the symbols of eternal suffering. Only after inscribing the story on its body can the stone stop "crying and lamenting day and night."

Here, the purpose of writing is not to express feelings but rather to experience them; and artistic creation is tantamount to the creation of a new way of living that replaces the act of shedding tears. In this sense, the stone is not only the bridge between the author and the hero, as well as between the human and the divine worlds within the novel, but also between writing and life, and between fiction and reality. The body of the stone is the very textuality of the novel.

The ambiguous division between the natural and supernatural world corresponds to the blurred distinction between "life" and "dream," as in the case of a famous anecdote of Chuang-tzu.

> In the past Chuang Chou dreamed he was a butterfly, spirits soaring he was a butterfly (is it that in showing what he was he suited his own fancy?), and ignorant of its existence as Chou. When all of a sudden he awoke, he was Chou with all his wits about him. He does not know whether he is Chou dreaming he is a butterfly or a butterfly dreaming he is Chou. Between Chou and the butterfly there is necessarily a dividing; this is what is meant by transformation of things.[12]

In this fable, Chuang-tzu shows that the division between truth and illusion—between reality and dream—exists only in the contradictory form of movable borders. One should, therefore, not waste time searching for a piece of solid ground on this shifting earth; rather one should enjoy one's identity even in illusions since, in the final analysis, truth and illusion are not separable.

To a large extent, the supernatural framework of *The Dream of the Red Chamber* owes its philosophical implications to the long interpretive tradition of Chuang-tzu's fable. This framework can be considered a variation on the "transformation of things" (*wu-hua*),[t] to use Chuang-tzu's terms. In this vein, the author even pretends that his novel is merely a dream.

> According to the author, after having experienced some dreams and illusions, he has dissimulated the truth and used the theory of the magic stone to write *The Story of the Stone*.[13]

If we take seriously what the author says here, this novel is doubly illusory: it is written on the basis of dreamlike experiences, the reality of which has been hidden. As with Chuang-tzu, truth and dream are confused and, in the end, identical. Insofar as they are distinguished at all, that distinction is not grounded as a fixed point in an external reality but as a movable point of transformation in a subjective sense.

But why conceal the truth of a dream? Perhaps because the very notion of "truth" is questionable, since it is based on subjective perception which is essentially unreliable. And perhaps this understanding of "truth" is the *only* truth, as the author may very well be pointing out in indicating the nature of the dream in the first poem: "The ancient as well as the modern worlds are a single dream of absurdity."

Thus the author's dream in this life becomes a double negation of reality, in which case it may be considered closer to "truth" than what we call "real life." This couplet in the Land of Illusion reappears throughout the book as a kind of refrain:

> Truth becomes fiction when the fiction's true;
> Real becomes not-real where the unreal's real . . . (1:1:55).

Ironically, therefore, because of the illusory nature of life, one needs to hide the truth of a dream, which is too authentic for the unauthentic world. Fiction can be more "real" than "reality," depending on the point of view.

If one views the entire novel as one long dream that strives to keep the truth hidden, there are still within this larger framework various shorter dreams. In parallel to the author's own experience, the hero has a long dream in the Land of Illusion from which the book takes its title, *The Dream of the Red Chamber*. The aspect of parallelism is revealed in the hero's dream as an allegorical interpretation of the author's experience of illusory life.

The dream starts with the appearance of the fairy Disenchantment, (*Ching-huan hsien-tzu*)[(Int.q)], or literally "the fairy who warns against illusion." In this case, there are at least four levels of illusion: the author's dream, the dream of the man named "hiding truth," the hero's dream in the Land of Illusion, and the land itself, which symbolizes the illusory fate of the hero and the girls of the garden. The novelistic world becomes a *mise en abyme* of illusion—that is illusion within illusion. It is again in the dream of the main character that the fairy appears in "the Illusory Land of Insubstantiality" (*t'ai-hsü huan-ching*).[(Int.t)]

The term (*ching-huan*)[u], "warning against illusion," has undertones of irony. Instead of warning the young hero against illusion, the fairy seems to be the very one who introduces him to illusion. One may object that this deed is a part of the process of enlightenment—that is, of the experience of the emptiness of worldly life in a Buddhist sense. But the result of the trip seems to cast her good will into doubt.

At the end of the dream when Pao-yü stands in front of "the Ford of Error" (*mi-chin*),[v] Disenchantment tells him:

> If you had gone on walking just now and had fallen in, all the good advice I was at such pains to give you, such as how to enlighten yourself through sentiment, how to conform to social norms, would have been wasted. (1:5:147)

Nevertheless, in his dream, the poor hero ends up precisely in this terrible ford. Ironically, he is "saved" from his nightmare by some beautiful maids from the so-called real world. Immediately after the dream, he makes love, for the first time in his life, with one of the maids, Hsi-jen. Even though the notion of the flesh is not as contemptible as in the case of the relationship between Julie and St. Preux in Rousseau's preromantic novel, this change, nonetheless, marks the end of Pao-yüeh's state of complete innocence. In other words, Pao-yü not only dreams of his fall but also realizes it in his waking life.

This dream is, at once, both the beginning of the book, since it introduces us to the world of the Chia family, and its ending since, in the poems as well as in the songs of this chapter, the fate of every character is already foretold. In this sense, the dream paradoxically reveals the truth of existential life. This beginning, in other words, is also the final destination.

Whereas Pao-yü's dream lays out an allegorical plan of the novel, Hsi-feng's dream at the moment of Ch'in K'e-ch'ing's[14] death emphasizes the human dimension of the family tragedy. K'e-ch'ing advises her friend about how to ensure the future of the Chia family. Not only is Hsi-feng her close friend, but she is also the strongest person in the large household of the Jung-kuo mansion. She is—or was, since it is difficult to tell if she is a living being or a ghost at this particular moment—in the Ning-kuo mansion.

Structurally, this advice is based on three "common sayings" (*su-yü*)[w] which describe the future of their family:

(1) The full moon smaller grows,
Full water overflows . . .

(2) The higher the climb,
The harder the fall . . .

(3) Even the best banquet must have an end . . . (1:13:257)

The message is unequivocal: not only is decline of the Chia family unavoidable in a personal sense, but such is the inexorable course of both the human and the natural worlds as well. Hsi-feng's preventive act suggested by K'e-ch'ing's good advice cannot alter fate. As K'e-ch'ing herself says in the dream:

Honor and disgrace follow each other in an unending cycle. No human power can arrest that cycle and hold it permanently in one position. (1:13:256)

This speech seems to contradict the very point of giving advice, for why bother to give it if one knows in advance that, in this natural course, nothing can be changed? Most likely the dream serves a different structural purpose in the novel; or more precisely, it contributes to the realistic level of the novel, which parallels the contribution of Pao-yü's dream to the symbolic level. Thus K'e-ch'ing, who is metamorphosed in the role of the sister of Disenchantment and plays the initiator of Pao-yü's sexual life in his dream, becomes the prophetess herself in Hsi-feng's dream.

Whereas the fairy Disenchantment uses metaphysical language to warn Pao-yü, the prince of the kingdom of girls—against worldly illusion in a transcendental world, here K'e-ch'ing as a human being hovering between life and death—uses three commonplaces to warn Hsi-feng, who is financially the most powerful person in the household, of the family's inevitable tragic end.

As the personification of sentiment (*ch'ing*) in a pun on both her family and first names, Ch'in K'e-ch'ing links each personal tragedy to the final dispersal of the family. Furthermore, because of her implied incestuous relationship with her father-in-law, this notion of "sentiment" is necessarily entangled with obscenity, which is considered as at the root of the family tragedy in Disenchantment's allegorical song. In this sense, K'e-ch'ing's presence in both dreams largely humanizes the Land of Illusion and gives the entire novel a strongly realistic impact. The shift from an allegedly divine language to earthly commonplaces moves in the same direction: from the insubstantial world to everyday life.

While Pao-yü is scared to death by the end of his famous dream and finds a kind of illusory happiness after waking up, the signal of death interrupts the apparently peaceful conversation between the two relatives and the close friends. A bell tolls in the darkness of night creating a supernatural but, at the same time, uncannily realistic atmosphere.

Hsi-feng has an intimate conversation in her dream with a living person who is dying at that very moment. Is this a dream or reality? Is it death or life?

As the incarnation of sentiment, Ch'in K'e-ch'ing represents the flesh in Disenchantment's spiritual domain and the prophetic figure in the Chia family's earthly setting; she is a living being in Hsi-feng's dream, and a dead person in the real world. To this extent, one may say that sentiment—or passion—is marginal in both the transcendent and material worlds, and in both life and death.

It can also be taken as, at the same time, superior and inferior to those various universes. Like Ch'in K'e-ch'ing's personality, the figure of sentiment is, first of all, ambiguous or indefinable. Her lucidity, like the different qualities of those sentimental beings in the novel, is limited to a passive prophecy of the disastrous future.

In using these impersonal commonplaces, Ch'in K'e-ch'ing seems to distance herself further from any personal responsibility for the prophecy. The qualities of those sentimental beings are not designed to "repair Heaven" nor to enhance the external situation but to exist "uselessly" or as objects of contemplation. This may partly explain their ambiguity, since they cannot simply be judged against moral standards. To this extent, they can be said to be beyond good and evil, as is the notion of sentiment itself in *The Dream of the Red Chamber.*

In this book, another dream is also connected to the hero's dream in the Land of Illusion. After the beautiful, dissolute, and passionate Yu San-chieh kills herself, Liu Hsiang-lien, her fiancé, deeply regrets his breaking off of the engagement. Guilt and sadness make him gradually lose consciousness.

Like K'e-ch'ing in Hsi-feng's dream, San-chieh also appears in her lover's dream to bid him farewell. She tells him that she is going:

> . . . to the fairy Disenchantment's tribunal in the Land of Illusion to keep the records of the other lovers who are under her jurisdiction. (3:66:306)

Hsiang-lien awakens from the illusory, other-worldly life, but, unlike Pao-yü, who upon awakening was initiated into sex, immediately becomes a Taoist monk. Why are two partially parallel dreams so different in their resolutions? One looks for an explanation in the contrast between Liu Hsiang-lien's coldness and Pao-yü's sentimentality.

But to a large extent, Hsiang-lien's apparent indifference is the proof of his own extreme sensitivity. He is almost Pao-yü's only close male friend, except for Ch'in Chung, K'e-ch'ing's brother (or in a pun, "seeds of passion," *ch'ing-chung*),[x] who dies at the beginning of the book. Furthermore, their friendship is based on a special reciprocal attachment to the "seed of passion" in the past.

As indicated in the ninth chapter, the relationship is rather questionable, since it provokes violent jealousy from other boys interested in homosexuality. Of course, the boy who has the ambiguous relationship with Ch'in Chung in this chapter is not directly named. He appears only under the nickname of "Darling" (*Hsiang-lien*)[y] which is perfectly homophonic with Liu Hsiang-lien. In this case, it is at least implied that both Pao-yü and Hsiang-lien are Ch'in Chung's lovers. This partnership makes each the mirror image of the other.

Therefore, one may consider Hsiang-lien's dream to encapsulate Pao-yü's personal experience: Hsiang-lien's ending foreshadows Pao-yü's final enlightenment. Pao-yü's dream, however, seems only to initiate him into sexual life, meaning that the true dream has not ended but has just begun. By making love with his maid, he is plunged more deeply into the dream, which is the illusory life itself.

These three dreams reveal different levels of truth about the Chia family and the Prospect Garden. Furthermore, the line of demarcation between dream and life is always blurred. In Pao-yü's case, life is the continuation or a simulacrum of his dream. Hsi-feng's dream ends in the realistic effect of a tolling bell. And Hsiang-lien's dream points out the meaning—or, more precisely, the emptiness—of life, not to mention the fact that the author (or the commentator) claims in the very first line that the whole book is only about experiences of dreams and illusions.

To a large extent, there is no absolute empirical, objective, or ethical truth, but only a subjective and aesthetic truth manifested in a concrete form "taste" (*wei*).[z] In a rhetorical question, the author admits that he doubts whether any of his readers will be able to understand this aesthetic truth. As the couplet in the Land of Illusion points out repeatedly:

> Truth becomes fiction when the fiction's true;
> Real becomes not-real when the unreal's real. (1:1:55)

Reflection of the Mind

Passion has an egoistic nature in both *Julie, ou la Nouvelle Héloïse* and *The Dream of the Red Chamber*. Whereas eroticism actively transgresses the society's behavioral norms, the exaltation of passion often marks an individual spiritual break with social conventions. This parallelism may explain the close tie between *Julie, ou la Nouvelle Héloïse* and *Les Liaisons dangereuses* as well as between *The Golden Lotus* and *The Dream of the Red Chamber*. The need to support one's ego in one's posture against society is partially satisfied by the idolatry of one's beloved, onto which one projects one's own value system. As we have seen in the first section of this chapter, the author of *The Dream of the Red Chamber* sometimes distorts the traditional meaning of a word; and in *The Golden Lotus*, one of the most important objects of transgression for the erotic hero is the relationship between "name" and "substance." By using the name of an adopted daughter to facilitate his sexual relationship with his so-called daughter, Hsi-men Ch'ing, the protagonist in *The Golden Lotus* violates Confucian values centered on family and based on the relationship between "name" and "substance." If the "rectification of names" (*cheng-ming*)[Chap. 2, s] occupies a central position in Confucius's writing, this is because names are considered to be the very embodiment of social authority.

In Hsün-tzu, for example, the name is supposedly established by the prince who governs the country.[15] Disregard of names is, therefore, tantamount to disregard of the social law. If Hsi-men Ch'ing's transgression of social law is more obvious and more brutal, the disrespect for "names" as words that is shown by the author of *The Dream of the Red Chamber*, though much more subtle, seems more subversive.

Chia Yü-ts'un, occasionally the author's spokesman, offers a theory to explain this individualism inherent in passion, based on his belief that, in this world, there are two opposite "forces" (*ch'i*).[aa]

> The generative process operating in the universe provides the great majority of mankind with natures in which good and evil comingled in more or less equal proportion. In-

stances of exceptional goodness and exceptional badness are produced by the operation of beneficent or noxious ethereal influences, of which the former are symptomized by the equilibrium of society and the latter by its disequilibrium. . . . The good cosmic fluid with which the natures of the exceptionally good are compounded is a pure, quintessential humor; whilst the evil fluid which infuses the natures of the exceptionally bad is a cruel, perverse humor. (1:2:66–67)

The two "essences" or "humors" in Hawkes's translation of (*ch'i*), have first of all a strong ethical undertone: "upright" (*cheng*)[bb] and "evil" (*hsieh*).[cc] Like the stones that the Goddess Nü-wa used to repair Heaven, these essences exist in the world only for the sake of collectivity. The distinction between them is based on their usefulness or harmfulness *vis-à-vis* society.

Normally, individualism emerges as an important ideology only after the line of demarcation between good and evil becomes blurred. This is precisely the case here, according to Yü-ts'un's explanation. He attributes the uselessness—or, more precisely, the loss of ethical values of the two essences—to the "peaceful and prosperous situation of the country."

This is a clever touch of irony on the part of the author in regard to the political situation. By chance, they may merge. Those who are born with a mixture of the two essences become the heroes of the book.

Such human recipients, whether they be male or female, since they are already amply endowed with the benign humor before the evil humor is infested, are incapable of becoming either greatly good or greatly bad; but place them in the company of ten thousand others and you will find that they are superior to all the rest in sharpness and intelligence and inferior to all the rest in perversity, wrongheadedness and eccentricity. Born into a rich or noble household they are likely to become great lovers or the occasion of great love in others. (1:1:78)

The originally ethical essences that can be used to save or to destroy the world become merely useless marks of distinction.

To make the useful useless is also a process of aestheticization of ethics, inasmuch as ethics imply responsibility toward society and aesthetics are free of constructive purpose. The characters in *The Dream of the Red Chamber,* most of whom are born into "a rich or noble household," manifest their "useless essence" mainly in "sentiment" (*ch'ing*). It goes without saying that "passion" or "sentiment" become the major objects of contemplation if we are to take Yü-ts'un as a reliable spokesman for the author in this context.

In any case, passion is inseparable from "stupidity" (*ch'ih*). These are the terms used by common people to qualify the singularity of certain main characters that they fail to understand. In this sense, "stupidity" may refer more to the one who judges than to the one who is judged, as in the case of "absurdity" (*huang-t'ang*).[dd] In the same vein, passion is the mark of distinction or individuality that common people mistakenly take as a symptom of inferiority, because it remains a value beyond their common sense. In this respect, the Chinese heroes resemble Rousseau's "sensitive souls."

Nevertheless, instead of ceaselessly proclaiming their own sensibilities as the French heroes in *Julie, ou la Nouvelle Héloïse* do, the Chinese heroes resort to a more indirect means of expression—that is, through the criticism of those whom they scornfully qualify as "worldly people" (*shih-jen*)[ee] or "vulgar people" (*su-jen*).

The less they are understood, the more distinguished they are. As the most "silly person" (*ch'ih-jen*)[ff] in the judgment of the worldly people, Pao-yü deserves—for this reason alone—to occupy the central position within the utopian garden, as a poem describes him:

> Oft-times he sought out what would make him sad;
> Sometimes an idiot seemed and sometimes mad.
> Though outwardly a handsome sausage-skin,
> He proved to have but sorry meat within.
> A harum-scarum, to all duty blind,
> A doltish mule, to study disinclined;
> His acts outlandish and his nature queer;
> Yet not a whit cared he how folk might jeer. (1:3:102)

Before this poem, the reader is oriented more to the perspective of Tai-yü, when she meets her cousin for the first time. Then, we shift to the viewpont of the narrator who adds an ironic undertone to Tai-yü's naive observation:

> In short, his outward appearance was very fine. But appearances can be misleading. (1:3:102)

The word "misleading" is, in itself, misleading since its irony may be directed to the naive admiration of Tai-yü for her handsome cousin as well as to the viewpont of "people in the future" (*hou-jen*).[gg] Since we are, by now, used to the author's paradoxical use of words, the next qualification in the poem—"very accurate"—may also be taken as a combination of double-perspectives. This "accurate" description of the hero according to the standards of the common people is likely to be unreliable because of the latters' lack of discernment.

This shifting of viewpoints is yet even more subtle in view of the fact that, in this poem, as in most Chinese classical poetry, all subjects are omitted. In this case, the subject "he" that Hawkes adds in his translation may sometimes mean "I" as a retroactive voice of the hero which is also identical with that of the author, thus lending an ambiguous self-mocking undertone to the text.

As in the first verse, "without reason" (*wu-ku*)[hh] can be interpreted as a marker of self-interrogation about the meaning of his own life. It can also be understood as the comments of the author, who borrows from the expressions of common people to point out ironically their failure to understand reason.

The second verse is apparently situated completely outside the hero, since he is viewed by others as a passive object. However, (*ssu*)[ii] and (*ju*)[jj] (both of which may be translated as "seemingly") provide a shade of irony that reveals the presence of the narrator's skeptical voice. In the third sentence, the qualifier "even though" (*ts'ung-jan*)[kk] refers, at the same time, to the reproach of people in the future and to a vague regret at a deeper level from the hero's retroactive point of view.

The last couplet is a typical hybrid construction: "his acts outlandish and his nature queer" is no doubt viewed from the perspective of the common people, who condemn the hero according to social conventions, whereas in the following verse the weapon is turned on them, their comments on the hero being rejected as "calumny" (*fei-pang*).[ll]

The narrator's expression "misleading" literally means "difficult to understand his ins and outs" (*nan-chih ti-ssu*).[mm] The pretendedly more "accurate" description of the poem further complicates "his truth" in offsetting those diversified or even contradictory points of view. The hero's personality takes on a strongly realistic aspect through the concatention of interpretations, because a real person is always multidimensional.

Later on, the remembered images combined with different perspectives serve as the background to which the book ceaselessly adds concrete information or expanded perspectives. We find this quality of multiple perspectives in many poems in the novel, especially in those describing personalities. And thanks to its rhyme and regular form, the poetic language intensifies images and marks them in our memory for future reference within the novel. Because of their combination of perspectives, most of the poems contribute to a complex horizon of individuality.

What is the concrete proof that Pao-yü's personality is characterized by "idiocy" (*sha*)[nn] and "craziness" (*k'uang*)?[oo] First of all, there is his special attachment to girls. In chapter 20, after describing Pao-yü's relationship with his brother, the narrator explains:

> But there was another zanier notion which contributed to this attitude. Let us try to explain it. Pao-yü had from early youth grown up among girls. . . . As a result of this upbringing, he had come to the conclusion that the pure essence of humanity was all concentrated in the female of the species and that males were its mere dregs and offscourings. To him, therefore, all members of his own sex without distinction were brutes who might just as well not have existed. (1:20:407–08)

"Stupid," "dull" (*tai*)[pp] and "idiotic" (*sha*) describe the hero's indifference toward social norms, especially the very fundamental belief in traditional China that girls are inferior. Indeed, according to Mencius, the worst of three transgressions of filial piety was not to have male descendants. By excluding himself from the male world, Pao-yü violates this ethical norm, since he rejects the responsibility of the heir who must assure the continuity of the family and society.

What he appreciates in his female cousins is their purity, which is essentially a negative quality or a "zero degree." Girls are useless creatures in society since they are not allowed to participate in any serious social activities. Their position in the human world is similar to the position of the stone in the divine world: useless. The glorification of the female world is equal to the condemnation of social authority, given the traditional paternalism of Chinese society. In this sense, the garden is an asylum of female tenderness into which he escapes from the world of male severity, as represented by his father.

This topological distance between girls and society, however, does not necessarily entail a fundamental difference between their personal judgment and the value system in society. The girls live in the Prospect Garden far removed from the filthiness of the outside world, not because of any active choice of their own. Rather, they are the passive "beneficiaries" of a situation that has been thrust upon them.

By contrast, Pao-yü's preference for the gynoecium is an active choice. Even though he is not a natural inhabitant of the garden, he is more faithful to this uptopian world than are most of the girls in it, since the garden is a macrocosm of his inner self.

St. Preux or Wolmar divinize Julie in order to idolize their subjective worlds, according to the belief that the one who *knows* is superior to the object of knowledge, and the one who *appreciates* is at least equal to the object of appreciation. In this active-passive relationship, "knowledge" as the basis of admiration still represents a form of power.

Contrary to the French characters, Pao-yü divinizes not one single girl but all members of the opposite sex in order to honor his own self. As the one who *knows* or *appreciates*, he places himself in a position higher than his favorite world of girls. As his nickname indicates, he is "the master of flowers in the Crimson Cave" (*Chiang-tung hua-chu*).[99] "Flowers" naturally represent the girls, and "the crimson cave" is no doubt a metaphor for the gynoecium, as in the case of "the red chamber."

Despite its location outside society, Pao-yü's subjective world as well as its incarnation—the Prospect Garden—cannot protect itself from external influences. First, Yü Ying-shi points out that the Garden's source of water is from the dirtiest part of the Chia family, the Mansion of Ning-kuo.[16] (Water is the symbol of the purity and innocence of the girls. As Pao-yü often says, "the girls are creatures made of water.")

Second, marriage as a social necessity marks the ephemeral character of this utopia. Like childhood, the garden is a transitory period. This is one of the reasons that Pao-yü refuses to grow up: to become an adult is to bid farewell to the refuge of his inner world.[17] The hero's fear for growing up implies an unwillingness to participate in social life. Therefore, it is not so surprising to see that the discussion about a girl's death may occasionally become enjoyable for the hero.

> We all have to die, as you said yourself just now. The problem is how to die well. Those whiskered idiots who take quite literally the old saying that "a scholar dies protesting and a soldier dies fighting" and get themselves killed off on the assumption that those are the only two ways in which a man of spirit can die gloriously, would do better to die in their beds. For when you come to think of it, the only real occasion for protesting is when one's country is at war. If the scholar is so greedy for martyrdom that he throws away his life at the earliest opportunity, what is to become of the poor misguided ruler in the absence of good advisers? And if the soldier so hankers for a hero's death that he gets himself killed off in the first encounter, what is to become of his country without soldiers to fight its battles? . . . . So you can see that all those death-with-honor characters you have so high an opinion of were thinking only of their own personal fame and glory. They weren't really thinking of their loyal duty to their sovereign at all.
>
> Now my idea of a glorious death would be to die now, while you are all around me; then your tears could combine to make a great river that my corpse could float away on, far, far away to some remote place that no bird has ever flown to, and gently decompose there until the wind had picked my bones clean, and after that never, never to be reborn again as a human being—that would be a really good death. (2:36:205–06)

By describing the difference between the most praiseworthy death in the eyes of common people—death for "name" or fame—and his own eventual death—which is idealized or poetized by its very uselessness—Pao-yü distinguishes two opposite attitudes toward life. In fact, it is easier for him to talk about death from that vantage point than about life.

Death prolongs forever his isolation in the garden and abolishes any control which society may have over him. Nevertheless, if death abolishes the restrictions of society, the existence of the garden as a refuge of his "self" also loses its *raison d'être*. In this case, a "nice" death would free him totally from the incarnation of his subjective projection as well as from the objective world.

By criticizing the way of dying respected and praised by common people, Pao-yü indirectly condemns the orthodox way of life in the same society. There were two major supports in traditional China—"scholarship" (*wen*)[rr] which represents the governing power, and "military arts" (*wu*)[ss] which represents the power protecting the government. The scholar-administrators and the warriors are supposed to act in accordance with Confucian morality—that is, to remain loyal to their duty and country even at the price of their own lives. In fact, to die for a moral cause is considered the highest honor in the Confucian tradition.

In mocking the Confucian scholars and military men who conform their actions to their "names" (*ming*)[tt] in order to gain "fame" (*ming*), the hero not only undermines the deeper truth of this morality but does so in playful language. To declare oneself against some social values is to confirm one's belief in certain other transindividual values, whereas relativization in playful language reveals an even more radical questioning of the notion of belief, be it orthodox or heterodox.

By shifting the target subtly from the part to the whole, Pao-yü has subverted the very foundations of society without even taking an explicitly political position. Very often, under the cover of his madness and stupidity, Pao-yü uses the same swerve to undermine something deeper than the apparent target.

This is one of the reasons that *The Dream of the Red Chamber* appears to be a more deeply subversive work than *The Golden Lotus:* the object of the subversion is the language itself. As Hayden White states:

> The very use of language itself implies or entails a specific posture before the world which is ethical, ideological, or more generally political.[18]

The author's subversive treatment of language cannot be ideologically neutral, neither in spite of nor because of its playfulness, since playfulness can also signal an ideological posture that challenges the reliability of the basis of transindividual values—a homogeneous language.

As we have noticed, Pao-yü's conception of death is equivalent to his conception of life. The happiness in his conception of death is deeply egotistical. He would not, for example, concern himself with the happiness or unhappiness of those whom he loves. On the contrary, their eventual suffering—represented by the image of the river of their tears—is taken as the supreme proof of their attachment to him and, therefore, would be the basis of his joy.

To this extent, one can find some similarities between him and Hsi-men Ch'ing. If the hero of *The Golden Lotus* wishes to possess all the women of this world physically—as his fifth wife, P'an Chin-lien, sarcastically points out—the hero of *The Dream of the Red Chamber* desires to possess them sentimentally.[19] In the case of the former, what is at stake is a dispersed bestial desire, whereas, in the case of the latter, it is the question of a strongly self-conscious narcissistic wish, the result of a sublimation of physical desire. If eroticism, in Georges Bataille's terms, is the transgression of social and individual norms,[20] spiritual love is not substantially different on this point from physical love—except that it is more presentable because of its desexualization.

As a man, Pao-yü can choose the female world as his utopia. The girls, however, do not necessarily participate in an active way in the values of the world in which they live, and which are, in part, Pao-yü's idealized inventions. Pao-yü himself is, from time to time, disappointed by the reactions of his female friends, especially Pao-ch'ai, who tries to convince him to follow the Confucian orthodox road by passing the imperial examination. He comments:

> "Why should a pure, sweet girl like you want to go imitating that ghastly crew of thievish, place-hunting career

worms," he would say, "bothering her head about 'fame' and 'reputation' and all that sort or rubbish? All these notions you are parroting were dreamed up by meddlesome old men in days gone before the express purpose of leading astray the whiskered idiots who came after them. I really think it's too bad that I should have to live in an age when the minds of nice, sensible girls are contaminated by such idiocies. It's a rank abuse of the intellectual gifts that you were born with. (2:36:195)

Even though the girls may not have participated actively in social life, this does not necessarily mean that they must reject all kinds of social values. On the contrary, very few of them consciously deny these values, such as "fame and gain" (*ming li*),[uu] and most of them essentially remain in a state of innocence— that is, they express no social consciousness whatsoever.

But the cleverest ones, thanks to their "intellectual gifts," can understand fairly well the value system of the outside world. Some of them, such as Pao-ch'ai, become a reverse mirror image of Pao-yü by choosing the values of the opposite sex—namely, fame and gain.

Therefore, there is a chiasmatic displacement of values. The men whom Pao-yü considers to be "dirty chaps with a beard" (*hsü-mei chuo-wu*)[vv] are "decent people" (*cheng-ching jen*)[ww] in the eyes of these girls, whereas the girls he takes as "pure and innocent" (*ch'ing-ching chieh-pai*)[xx] are useless in their own eyes. If he regrets the "rank abuse of (their) intellectual gifts" (*chung-ling yü-hsiu*),[yy] Pao-ch'ai and her kind may also regret the waste of his male talent, which is supposed to be used to acquire fame and interest.

Because of this gap between their perceptions, Pao-yü and Pao-ch'ai will never be able to deal seriously with ethical issues from the same point of view despite their mutual attraction based on "intellectual gifts" and physical beauty. This difference in value systems prevents Pao-yü from loving Pao-chai or any other girls as much as he loves Tai-yü, although the two cousins are equally beautiful and intelligent.

This emphasis on internal similarity and on a comparable value system between the lovers distinguishes *The Dream of the*

Red Chamber from most other traditional Chinese novels dealing with the same subject. In this novel, "sentiment" *ch'ing* is a much more complicated and individualized concept than "sentiment" portrayed in the so-called "romance of talented young men and beautiful girls" (*ts'ai-tzu chia-jen hsiao-shuo*).[zz] In most of these "romances" love is equal to an abstract formulation in which the woman seeks talent and the man seeks beauty invariably. In fact, in spite of Pao-yü's weakness for all the girls in the garden, only one, Tai-yü, can be taken as the mirror image of Pao-yü's self, because she consciously shares his contempt for conventional values:

> The exception was Tai-yü, who, ever since they were little children together, had never once spoken to him about the need to "get on in the world" or "make a name for oneself." This was why he so much respected her. (2:36:195)

Passion finds its justification in an exaltation of the self. Whereas in *Julie, ou la Nouvelle Héloïse,* a sensitive soul suffers because of its inadequacy in the world, in *The Dream of the Red Chamber* the very criticism leveled against the common people for their failure to understand the heroes' distinguished essence proves the distinction of the object of their criticism. In this regard, the French novel analyzes sensibility as a mark of difference and portrays it from a subjective point of view, perhaps thanks to the Christian tradition's emphasis of the study of "self" as an image of God—albeit as a dispersed image.

The Chinese case describes the same difference indirectly—perhaps more objectively—through the refracted vision of others. In other words, criticism or calumny is the homage paid to these narcissistic heroes whose superiority lies in their distinguished natures, which is beyond the understanding of common people. T'u Ying points out that "One can judge *The Dream* only according to sentiment, not according to reason."[21]

In chapter 57, Tzu-chüan tests Pao-yü's loyalty to her mistress, Tai-yü. Pao-yü's reaction outstrips the maid's expectations. Tzu-chüan hopes the young master is shocked, he is indeed so shocked that he completely loses his reason for the moment. After the girl jokingly lied to him that Tai-yü is going to leave his family, Pao-yü almost dies and then becomes truly crazed. (3:57:96–97) There is an undercurrent of seriousness in this humorous passage. Pao-yü's ridiculous symptoms of madness reveal incomparable sincerity while in the throes of his passion. Pao-yü's madness in this instance is the highest expression of passion because, in making a fool of himself, he runs afoul of all common sense. He no longer confines himself within the limitations of reality. The toy boat, for example, becomes more real than reality as the threatening symbol of losing Tai-yü. Pao-yü in his madness sees this boat as a "real" one, which will take Tai-yü from him. Consequently, he hides this boat in his bed, under his quilt as a guarantee of Tai-yü's permanent stay in his household, or more precisely as the surrogate of Tai-yü's body. Game and reality are not only undistinguishable but also reversible. Pao-yü's temporary madness here is not the distortion of his nature but its fullest manifestation. In other words the two lovers can be separated only at the price of their reason and life. This will truly happen at the end of the novel. In this sense, Pao-yü here is unconsciously playing his future self—that is, what he will be when Tai-yü's departure from the human world is turned into a hopeless reality.

There is yet more to this scene of Pao-yü's passion: it is also a manifestation of the egocentric nature of this passion. In spite of his theory of female superiority, girls—including his favorite cousin—are, in his eyes, equal to precious objects. And however sensitive he ordinarily appears toward Tai-yü's sadness—caused by the awareness of her solitude and her unavowed passion for Pao-yü—deep within his self, he would like to possess Tai-yü exclusively, as her only close relative and as her lover. In this sense, any other relatives of his favorite cousin could emotionally as well as legally threaten his monopoly on her.

It is significant that Pao-yü, in the throes of madness, takes the small self-propelling boat as the one in which Tai-yü will sail to her hometown. The expensive toy and the beautiful cousin are identical in the mind of the adolescent. By hiding the boat under his quilt, Pao-yü believes that Tai-yü will never be able to leave him. Ironically, she becomes his "possession," just like the expensive exotic toy—hidden in his bed.

Moreover, Pao-yü's situation as the cherished heir of the family is no less ridiculous. His whimsical demand must be sat-

isfied without the slightest delay. His grandmother, the most authoritative figure in the mansion, even begs her servants to
follow his zaniest request: "Please listen to me this time, my children!" The servants want to laugh, not necessarily at Pao-yü's
madness but at the grandmother's unreasonable love for the heir.

Lu Hsün, the famous modern Chinese writer, is no doubt
right in pointing out—sarcastically as usual—that "The servant
Chiao Ta in the Chia family will not fall in love with sister Lin."[22]
To a large extent, Pao-yü's passion can only survive in these special circumstances of excessive love. All its subtlety can be taken
as the fantasy of the spoiled child of a rich family, if the reader
identifies himself or herself with the servants—as the text per-
mits him or her to do in some cases.

The scene of Pao-yü's madness offers an ambivalent picture
of the nature of his passion. On the one hand, the absurdity of
Pao-yü's passion results from the misunderstanding of his exceptional essence by the common people. On the other hand,
this distinguished essence is inseparable from certain extravagant
circumstances, which later on bring about the destruction of
the family.

Is his passion praiseworthy or blameworthy? This question
is extremely difficult to answer. However, what is most fascinat-
ing in *The Dream of the Red Chamber* is the openendedness of
its contradictions.

For example, the polarity of "distinguished" and "common" is paralleled by that of "fanciful" and "reasonable," as
in Pao-yü's madness observed by the servants in the mansion. In
terms of conflicts of value systems, it is difficult, if not impossible, to judge which one is superior to the other. Each system
can be considered as "good" depending on from which angle
you view it.

If the world of passion is used to criticize the "real" world,
the latter eventually takes revenge. Even negations cancel each
other out, to the extent that no value system can be considered
predominant.

Whereas in *The Golden Lotus*, the excessive desire of Hsi-men
Ch'ing is as much evil as ugly, Pao-yü's world of passion is beautiful and sublime, even if it symbolizes a destructive and self-
destructive force bordering on craziness. Unlike the lovers in
Rousseau's novel, who exalt passion to the point of religious wor-

ship, no matter how passionate these Chinese adolescents are, their love remains mainly of the human world, in spite of the protection afforded by the utopian garden. The exaltation of passion is always tempered and counterbalanced by other value systems, which gently turn the exaltation into something close to an object of derision, even though the value systems themselves may be more laughable than what they laugh at.

Communication of Love by Means of Its Negation

To a large extent, the misunderstanding between the two lovers in *The Dream of the Red Chamber* is determined by the nature of the Chinese language and literature: it lacks the kind of a well-formed and respectable rhetoric of love that is found for example, in eighteenth-century French literature. How then could one express love while, at the same time, avoiding the pitfall of appearing lustful in an ordinary sense? This is a difficult task not only for the young hero but even for the experienced author. In this case, the use of playful language does not necessarily indicate detachment. It may indicate instead the author's seriousness, because the usual language is not serious enough to describe true love. The Chinese novelist, lacking language to express his (or his heroes') passion, must use his ingenuity to devise a substitute.

Let us consider the case of quarrelsome language. If one calculates the number of quarrels between Pao-yü and Tai-yü, they add up to an impressive portion of the novel. Moreover, quarrels are considered as proof of their mutual attachment.

> As for Pao-yü, he was still only a child—a child, moreover, whom nature had endowed with the eccentric obtuseness of a simpleton. Brothers, sisters, cousins, were all one to him. In his relationships with people he made no distinction between one person and another. If his relationship with Tai-yü was a little bit closer, it was because living with him in his grandmother's quarters made her more familiar to him than the rest; and greater familiarity bred greater intimacy. And of course, with greater intimacy came the occasional tiffs and misunderstandings that are usual with people who have a great deal to do with each other. (1:5:124–25)

"Childhood" (*hai-t'i*),[aaa] "inner nature" (*t'ien-hsing*),[bbb] and "obtuseness" (*yü-chuo*)[ccc] point out the hero's unawareness of his own feelings at the beginning of his relationship with his cousin. The relationship does not appear, even to himself, to be different from that usually found between juvenile cousins—except perhaps for the excessive number of quarrels. Therefore, there seems to be a touch of innocence in his attachment.

In this context of the "drawback of perfectionism" (*Ch'iu-ch'üan chih-hui*)[ddd] and the "unpredictable conflicts" (pu-yü chih-hsi),[eee] quarrels remain the only means by which to express their mutual attachment. What is *really* at stake is the perfection of their relationship through a complete mutual understanding. But, lacking an adequate language with which to describe their feelings and without a suitable discourse of love, they cannot even understand their own feelings, let alone know how to express them.

Misunderstanding is therefore unavoidable, although that astonishes the two adolescents. Their intentions are so sincere, yet the result is failed communication. Paradoxically, and thanks to those misunderstandings, they come to understand their own and each other's feelings much better with the quarrels, for want of something more suitable yet providing an indirect but efficient way in which to express their love.

In the West in general, a long tradition fortified by Christianity endows spiritual passion with a noble nature. As the sublimated form of sensuality, love implies the exclusion of a sinful body.

In *Julie, ou la Nouvelle Héloïse*, for example, the heroine confuses her devotion to God with her passion for her lover. What Julie and St. Preux need to overcome is not their chaste love but rather the desire of their evil bodies, on the grounds that love that emancipates itself from physical attraction consists precisely of the best part of their inner world.

In *The Dream of the Red Chamber*, genuine love also belongs only to the "noble essence," but the former cannot be the latter's justification or achieve its elevation. Love always has an ambiguous nature. First of all, a precise definition is lacking in Ts'ao's novel. The Chinese equivalent expression of love (*ai*)[(Int.m)] is never used in the novel to describe the mutual relationship between the lovers.

On the contrary, the erotic hero of *The Golden Lotus* uses the same word fairly often to describe his physical fondness for a part of the body of a woman (such as hands, legs, skin, and so on). However, in *The Dream of the Red Chamber*, the fairy Disenchantment gives an authoritative definition of Pao-yü's passion (*ch'ih-ch'ing*)[fff] by the use of another word, "obscenity" or "lust" (*yin*)[Int.P], which has numerous pejorative connotations in the Chinese language.[23]

After telling Pao-yü the reason why she likes him—he is "the most lustful person in this world"—the fairy continues with her explanation of lust:

> In principle, of course, all lust is the same. But the word has many different meanings. For example, the typically lustful man in the common sense of the word is a man who likes a pretty face, who is fond of singing and dancing, who is inordinately given to flirtation; one who makes love in season and out of season, and who, if he could, would like to have every pretty girl in the world at his disposal, to gratify his desires whenever he felt like it. Such a person is a mere brute. His is a shallow, promiscuous kind of lust.
>
> But your kind of lust is different. That blind, defenseless love with which nature has filled your being is what we call "lust of the mind." "Lust of the mind" cannot be explained in words, nor, if it could, would you be able to grasp their meaning. Either you know what it means or you don't.
>
> Because of this "lust of the mind" women will find you a kind and understanding friend; but in the eyes of the world I am afraid it is going to make you seem impractical and eccentric. It is going to earn you the jeers of many and the angry looks of many more. (1:5:146)

How one interprets the significance of this definition depends on how one understands the role of the fairy Disenchantment. As the one in charge of the Land of Illusion—which is tantamount to the supernatural representation of the world of the girls or the garden—she and her kingdom symbolize both the fate and the spirit of these girls. Since Pao-yü is the master of the kingdom of the girls, the fairy is closely related to the hero.

Taking into account the autobiographical aspect of the novel, the fairy can be considered the supernatural spokeswoman who reflects most intimately the opinion of the author. But what is that opinion?

First, she denies the distinction between "sentiment" (*ch'ing*) and "lust" (*yin*), by saying that this is merely another illusion. Both sensuality and sentiment have their common root in lust or excessive sexual desire. That being the case, there should be no qualitative difference between so-called "spiritual" and "physical" love since, after all, the *spiritual* is also *physical*. But the fairy seems to contradict herself in differentiating "meaning," (*yi*)[ggg] within the same category of lust in her statement of "All lust results from the same principle, but it has different meanings." (1:5:146)

Nevertheless, one can still make some coherent sense of it if one understands "principle" (*li*)[hhh] as the deepest motivation of love as lust, and "meanings" (*yi*) as the different understandings and interpretations of the same motivation. Then, "meanings" (*yi*) become different manifestations of the same "principle" (*li*) of "lust" (*yin*).

If the fairy distinguishes Pao-yü's kind of lust from the ordinary kind, it is not because the former is better than the latter in terms of essence, but rather because the former is more refined and more sophisticated than the latter in terms of form. In contrast to the Western distinction between the body and the soul in love, "the lust of the mind" is less tolerable in the eyes of the world and more damnable in terms of common morality because of its uncanniness, as the fairy explains "it is going to earn you the jeer of many and the angry looks of many more." (1:5:146)

This ambiguous distinction reminds us of another definition by probably the most enthusiastic defender of passion in the Chinese tradition—T'ang Hsien-tsu, the author of *The Peony Pavilion*, the play that awakens the awareness of love in the mind of our two adolescent lovers. The playwright writes in the preface to his work:

> The events of the human world cannot be fully understood in the human world. They are not men of great wisdom,

how can they generally categorize those events with human reason! If I know that reason does not exist, how can I be sure if passion really exists?[24]

Both the supernal agent of Ts'ao and the self-apologetic voice of T'ang describe passion negatively, in terms of what it is not. One defines it in opposition to the usual kind of lust; the other, to reason. But both believe that passion is the superior notion. But why?

Neither Ts'ao Hsüeh-ch'in, who speaks through his supernatural agent, nor T'ang Hsien-tsu, in the defense of his own work, can find a suitable answer.

The "shallow, promiscuous lust" (*p'i-fu lan-yin*)[(Int.s)] can be translated more literally as the lust of the flesh. In spite of her refusal to distinguish love from lust, the fairy still sets up a dichotomy between the flesh and the mind. This line of demarcation is neither metaphysical nor ethical. But, again, it is aesthetic.

The lust of common people emphasizes usefulness. They "use" female beauties to satisfy their desire of the moment, whereas Pao-yü's admiration of female beauty is an aimless enjoyment. What he desires is not a concrete return but to become a "kind and understanding friend of the girls" (*kui-ke chih-yu*).[iii]

The fairy describes in detail the common kind of lust. This reminds us of Hsi-men Ch'ing, the hero of *The Golden Lotus*, who desires "to have every pretty girl in the world at his disposal." But these descriptions can refer to a much wider literary category, including two other literary genres, namely, erotic novel and romance of talented young men and beautiful girls, that had a strong influence on *The Dream of the Red Chamber*; as the stone explains at the beginning of the book.

> Still worse is the "erotic novel," by whose filthy obscenities our young folk are all too easily corrupted. And the "romances of talented young men and beautiful girls," those dreary stereotypes with their volume after volume all pitched on the same note and their different characters undistinguishable except by name (all those ideally beautiful young ladies and ideally eligible young bachelors)—even they seem unable to avoid descending sooner or later into indecency (or lust).

Novels about the relationship between man and woman, called erotic or romantic prevailing in the same period, are damnable in the eyes of the brother Stone for their "indecency" or "lust" (*yin-lan*)[jjj] They belong to Disenchantment's category of "shallow, promiscuous lust." Interestingly enough, as the voice of narrator, the stone does not state in positive terms how it treats the same problem in its own story. What the Stone does is to process by negation, to tell the reader that *The Dream of the Red Chamber* differs from the other works on this point, in the way that the fairy defined Pao-yü's lust.

> It can be understood by the heart but not explained in words; it can be communicated by spiritual movements not by linguistic expressions. (1:5:146)

In characterizing the lust of the mind as linguistically uncommunicable, the fairy spares herself any further descriptions of its nature and leaves the poor reader forever puzzled.

How can love be based on sexual desire and at the same time exclude any physical utilitarianism? This contradiction cannot be resolved either by the fairy Disenchantment or by the brother Stone, and not even by the famous playwright of passion T'ang Hsien-tsu since it stems, first of all, from an indeterminancy of the Chinese language. (*Ai-ch'ing*)[Int.l], which is the modern Chinese equivalent of the Western "love," seems to be an invention of the late nineteenth century and especially from translations of Western novels. (*Ai*)[Int.m] in *The Dream of the Red Chamber* has a more material resonance, as in "caring about things" (*ai-wu*)[Int.n]. The expression "ai" in this novel has little to do with its modern word "love."

For this reason Pao-yü's love, or his "lust of the mind," always borders on obscenity, no matter how hard he (or the author, or the spokesmen of the author) tries to prove to the contrary. This linguistic ambiguity is one of the sources of numerous quarrels between the two adolescent lovers. However, this necessity is also a form of freedom. As Harold Bloom affirms;

> Freedom, in a poem, must mean freedom of meaning, the freedom to have a meaning of one's own. Such freedom is

wholly illusory unless it is achieved against a prior pleni-
tude of meaning, which is tradition, and so also against
language.[25]

In Bloom's terms, poetic freedom becomes a "combat of meaning
against meaning." Also, "a strong reading" which affirms the
poetic self is always "a misreading." The moment of a strong
reading is somewhat evasive; the old form has been broken, and
the new one is not necessarily formulated yet. This is precisely
the case of "lust"(*yin*) in *The Dream of the Red Chamber.*

Since no previous concept of love seemed to be exactly the
same as what the author of *The Dream of the Red Chamber* wanted
to express in his novel, he had to invent a new notion which is
the very proof of his freedom. But, at the same time, a new linguistic concept cannot be created totally out of nothing. The invention is necessarily limited by the old meaning from which the
new one departs.

A reader of *Julie, ou la Nouvelle Héloïse* must remember how
the quotations of previous literary texts help the lovers to express
successfully their feelings and even add to their passion. However, in the case of *The Dream of the Red Chamber*, previous literary
quotations seem to hinder the communication between the lovers. The most quoted works, other than Chuang-tzu, are indeed
about love. They are two plays, *The West Chamber*[26] (*Hsi-hsiang
chi*)[kkk] and *The Peony Pavilion (Mou-tan t'ing)*[Int.32,w].

Pao-yü and Tai-yü can each appreciate the plays. But when
they try to use the language they have learned from the plays
as a means of communication, it inevitably leads to misunderstandings.

For example, when Pao-yü and Tai-yü read these forbidden
books together, the former—perhaps deeply moved by the play
and by the fact that his emotion is shared by his beloved—makes
a joke to Tai-yü by quoting the expressions of their book:

> "Well" said Pao-yü, "is it good?"
> Tai-yü smiled and nodded. Pao-yü laughed.
> "How can I, full of sickness and of woe, withstand
> that face which kingdoms could overthrow?"
> Tai-yü reddened to the tips of her ears. The eyebrows
> that seemed to frown yet somehow didn't were raised now

in anger and the lovely eyes flashed. There was rage in her crimson cheeks and resentment in all her looks.

"You're hateful!"—she pointed a finger at him in angry accusal—"deliberately using that horrible play to take advantage of me. I'm going straight off to tell Uncle and Aunt!"

At the words "take advantage of me" her eyes filled with tears, and as she finished speaking she turned from him and began to go. (1:23:464)

Even though Rousseau might believe that one ought to forbid an unmarried girl to read his *Julie, ou la Nouvelle Héloïse,* reading love novels was still a fashionable thing to do in the upper classes of eighteenth-century France. This would have been all right if Julie had been content with idolizing passion in a literary context. Her behavior becomes "indecent" only at the moment in which she wants to substitute herself for the passionate novelistic heroine. But, as a novelistic heroine herself, her passion is again admired and accepted by the Parisian upper-class society.

In the context of *The Dream of the Red Chamber,* passion is a much more problematic notion even as an aesthetic object. Passion can be admired as an object of amusement or of entertainment on stage—that is, in public. To privately read plays about passion, as Pao-yü and Tai-yü do, is already to sin against decorum since it implies a sensual relationship between the reader and the text, which also implies the same between the two readers. In fact, as Wong Kam-ming points out in his dissertation, this scene is the ideal setting for the awakening of their romantic feelings for each other through a search for linguistic definition.[27] But merely to pay attention to the meaning of songs in such a play, as Tai-yü does in the same chapter, is again considered shameful.

This social contempt for sensual desire, somehow internalized in Tai-yü's way of thinking, leads to an overly keen sense of shame. In a sense, love is always linguistic, determined or even created by linguistic expressions. The very proof is that the lovers in *The Dream of the Red Chamber* only begin to understand themselves after reading romances. Language is the only means they have of formulating—and thus sublimating—their formless and unavowed desire.

Nevertheless, love cannot become an idealized object of worship unless it can be separated from sexual craving, which is always to a degree "anticivilized" and "anticultural."[28] In this sense, sexual craving is against the self-idolatry of the lovers, who portray themselves as the most beautiful and lovable of creatures. However much the lovers believe themselves to be superior to conventional society, their superiority must be based on an implicit recognition or even a secret admiration on the part of the same society. Since the notion of comparison only exists within society, no criteria of comparison can be purely individualistic. Therefore, the puritanical code of Confucian society, which may apparently be ignored by the heroes, is no less internalized in the form of shame. In fact, the sublimation of sexual desire usually leads the lovers toward a purification of the elements that are considered indecent or shameful in accordance with certain societal conventions.

What particularly angers Tai-yü about the two expressions quoted by Pao-yü are their sexual implications. In this sense, even though the language of romantic plays comes closest to what the two adolescents need in order to describe their feelings, it remains hopelessly inadequate in this task because of its ambiguous connections with the flesh.

Some commentators on *The Dream of the Red Chamber* reproach Tai-yü for her skeptical and possessive nature. But if we put any of them in the same situation, probably their behaviors would not have been much different. Tai-yü plays a much more difficult role than her lover. If a simple joke of Tai-yü's maid about her eventual departure makes Pao-yü lose his reason (3:57:96–97), what about living under the daily pressure and constant danger of losing the object of his love as Tai-yü does? Pao-yü's "love for those who do not love" (*ch'ing pu ch'ing*)[lll] is not in any sense universal love. It is certainly not less possessive and exclusive than Tai-yü's "love for those who love her" (*ch'ing ch'ing*).[mmm]

Pao-yü's situation is much better than that of Tai-yü. First, he can transfer his affection to many other girls, cousins as well as maids. Second, Pao-yü does not need to internalize his love as much as Tai-yü does, given that Chinese traditional society was much more tolerant in terms of virtue toward its male members than toward their opposite sex. Third, Pao-yü is the cherished male heir of the family, the "phoenix" (*feng-huang*)[nnn] of the household,[29] whereas Tai-yü lives under the roof of her relatives, dependent upon the affection of her maternal grandmother.

However, since Tai-yü's feeling is expressed only in spite of her self-consciousness and resistance to a language associated with sensuality, such expressions, rare as they are, become more natural and more powerful. In a sense, both Pao-yü and Tai-yü must invent a new language to describe their passion. The invention is accomplished gradually through their resistance to the old language, their hesitation, and their pitiful quarrels.

Chapter 32 provides the only scene in which the lovers try seriously to express their love in an explicit language. Since Tai-yü has overheard Pao-yü's favorable comments on her in comparison with Pao-ch'ai, she is in a mood to trust his speech. Especially after unwittingly making a joke about the relationship between him and her potential rival, Pao-ch'ai, she is wary of making him unnecessarily anxious again. In order to understand their language, we should look closely at a scene that recounts a successful communication:

> She moved forward and wiped the perspiration from his brow. For some moments he stood there motionless, staring at her. Then:
> "Don't worry!"
> Hearing this, Tai-yü herself was silent for some moments.
> "Why should I worry?" She said eventually. "I don't understand you. Would you mind telling me what you are talking about?"
> Pao-yü sighed: "Do you really not understand? Can I really have been all this time mistaken in my feeling towards you? If I don't know your mind, it's small wonder that you're always getting angry on my account."
> "I really don't understand what you mean about not worrying," said Tai-yü.
> Pao-yü sighed again and shook his head.
> "My dear coz, don't think you can fool me. If you don't understand what I've just said, then not only have my feelings towards you been all along mistaken, but all that you have ever felt for me has been wasted, too. It's because

you worry so much that you've made yourself ill. If only you could take things a bit easier, your illness wouldn't go on getting more and more serious all the time."

Tai-yü was thunderstruck. He had read her mind—had seen inside her more clearly than if she had plucked out her entrails and held them out for his inspection. And now there were a thousand things that she wanted to tell him; yet though she was dying to speak, she was unable to utter a single syllable and stood there like a simpleton, gazing at him in silence. (2:32:132)

In this conversation, "heart' " or "mind" (*hsin*)°°° is the central term, repeated more than ten times. (*Fang-hsin*)ᴾᴾᴾ literally means to set one's mind at rest. Pao-yü's request that Tai-yü set her mind at rest is also a request for her understanding of his mind or, more precisely, his heart—the source of love. In fact, what Tai-yü worries about most is the nature of his feeling for her.

If there is a latent competition between Tai-yü and Pao-ch'ai in regard to their male cousin, it functions at two different levels. What interests Tai-yü is to be the first one in Pao-yü's heart; thus she emphasizes the internal and idealistic aspect of their relationship.

On the other hand, Pao-ch'ai concentrates her energy on its external and practical aspect in pleasing people who will decide Pao-yü's fate. Since the antagonism between the hero and external authority is unresolvable, neither of his two cousins can win the battle. Even though the ending remains a riddle for us because of the two different authorships, it is certain that Tai-yü cannot marry Pao-yü without family support or the support of "worldly people," whereas Pao-ch'ai, even after the marriage, cannot live happily without love. As the prophetic poem indicates in Pao-yü's dream;

> Even with a wife so courteous
> that she holds the dinner tray
> to the height of her eyebrow,
> There could be no comfort
> for my afflicted heart."

Pao-yü's answer to Tai-yü's question in the quoted passage seems clumsy, but it is in reality a *tour de force*. If the language is not powerful enough, it probably never will be and he will never be able to overcome Tai-yü's suicidal skepticism. Instead of answering, he asks a rhetorical question. "You really don't understand me?"

If the question is more efficiently affirmative than an affirmation in this case, the affirmation in his answer is turned into a question.

First of all, the negation becomes a confirmation. "Since I *really* know your *mind,* then why are you always getting angry at me?" Tai-yü's two conflicting voices become weaker, but she still urges more confirmation in repeating again the word *"fang-hsin."*

Pao-yü seems more confident in his second answer by setting up a mirror image of the hearts of the two lovers. In other words, "I cannot describe my heart, but mine is exactly like yours." *Hsin* in "our intention" and "our feeling"*(yung-hsin)*[qqq] *(tai-wo chih-hsin)*[rrr], is no longer passive, but active. It implicitly indicates their love for each other. "Our hearts are similar because they feel the same attraction to each other." In pointing out the source of her sickness—"unable to set her heart to rest" (*pu fang-hsin*)[sss]—Pao-yü reveals his own understanding of her heart, which results from his attachment (*yung-hsin*) through a reflective game of the mind.

In other words, "Our minds are identical. If I understand you so well, it is through my mind, why are you unable to understand me through yours?" This underlying statement corresponds to Disenchantment's definition of "the lust of Mind"—"it can be understood by the heart but not explained in speech. It can be communicated through souls but not through language."[31] St. Preux uses the same strategy to convince Julie in asking her to consider her own heart as a guarantor of his affection; whereas the libertine Valmont, probably inspired by *Julie, ou la Nouvelle Héloïse,* also asks Tourvel to look at her heart in order to trust his in *Les Liaisons dangereuses.* But the difference is that this reflective function of heart becomes the only means of communication in the Chinese novel, whereas in the two French novels, it is simply one element of a series of rhetoric of love.

Love is wordless. It can only be mirrored in the heart of each lover through a gesture of appeal and response, not with language but with the similarity of their feelings. What is at stake is a vision of the mind that can be grasped only by a mind possessing the same vision, since it is through its own vision that the one mind understands that of the other. In this case, not only does the beloved become the mirror image of the "self," but the essence of "love" is turned into a narcissistic feature.

Far from Rousseau's lovers who resort to writing in order to create a past happiness that will reinforce their love, the Chinese adolescents must express their love in *spite* of language, in a metaphorical way that deforms language, or in a suggestive way such as poetry. In this sense, the expression of true love in *The Dream of the Red Chamber* is always a breaking of linguistic form, a "*cri de coeur*"—to use a Rousseauist expression.

Appendix of Chinese Characters

Introduction

a. 金瓶梅

b. 紅樓夢

c. 小說

d. 章回小說

e. 三國演義

f. 西遊記

g. 水滸

h. 儒林外史

i. 格物

j. 致良知

k. 氣

l. 愛情

m. 愛

n. 愛物

o. 情

p. 淫

q. 警幻仙子

r. 意淫

s. 皮膚濫淫

t. 太虛幻境

u. 狂

v. 傻

w. 牡丹亭

Chapter 2

a.	報	m.	手段
b.	到手	n.	慶
c.	雌兒	o.	馨
d.	值得	p.	號
e.	一面	q.	四泉
f.	說着	r.	三泉
g.	西天老聖僧	s.	正名
h.	慕	t.	君君，臣臣，　父父，
i.	清		子子。
j.	念頭	u.	魂飛魄散
k.	善	v.	楚雲
l.	咱閨那	w.	狂風驟雨

Chapter 4

a.	靈性，　靈氣	g.	空空道人
b.	名實	h.	大荒
c.	荒唐言	i.	無稽
d.	俗人	j.	癡
e.	大觀園	k.	天子
f.	石兄	l.	青埂

m.	情根		gg.	後人
n.	真事隱		hh.	無故
o.	案		ii.	似
p.	偶		jj.	如
q.	三生石		kk.	縱然
r.	密青果		ll.	誹謗
s.	辛酸淚		mm.	難知底細
t.	物化		nn.	傻
u.	警幻		oo.	狂
v.	迷津		pp.	呆
w.	俗語		qq.	絳洞花主
x.	情種		rr.	文
y.	香憐		ss.	武
z.	味		tt.	名
aa.	氣		uu.	名利
bb.	正		vv.	鬚眉濁物
cc.	邪		ww.	正經人
dd.	荒唐		xx.	清淨潔白
ee.	世人		yy.	鍾靈毓秀
ff.	痴人		zz.	才子佳人小說

aaa .	孩提		kkk .	西廂記
bbb .	天性		lll .	情不情
ccc .	愚拙		mmm .	情情
ddd .	求全之毀		nnn .	鳳凰
eee .	不虞之隙		ooo .	心
fff .	癡情		ppp .	放心
ggg .	意		qqq .	用心
hhh .	理		rrr .	待我之心
iii .	閨閣之友		sss .	不放心
jjj .	淫濫			

Notes

Introduction

1. Georges Bataille, *Erotism: Death and Sensuality*, trans. Mary Dalwood (San Francisco: City Lights, 1986), 256.

2. As Jacques Lacan states: "The object of desire, in common sense, is either a phantasm, which is in reality the support of desire, or a trap." Jacques Lacan, *Les Quatre Concepts fondamentaux de psychanalyse* (Paris: Seuil, 1964), 168.

3. Jean-Jacques Rousseau, *Julie, ou La Nouvelle Héloïse, Oeuvres complètes*, vol. 2 (Paris: Gallimard, "Pléiade," 1959). *Julie, or the New Eloise*, translated and abridged by Judith H. McDowell (University Park: Pennsylvania State University Press, 1968).

4. Choderlos de Laclos, *Les Liaisons dangereuses, Oeuvres complètes* (Paris: Gallimard, "Pléiade," 1979). Choderlos de Laclos, *Dangerous Acquaintances*, trans. Richard Aldington (Norfolk: James Laughlin, 1952).

5. Lan-ling Hsiao-hsiao sheng, *Chin P'ing Mei tz'u-hua* (*The Golden Lotus*), five volumes (Tokyo: Dai-an, 1963).

6. Ts'ao Hsüeh-ch'in, (or Cao Xue-qin) and kao E, *Hung-lou meng (san-chia p'ing-pen)*, four volumes. (Shanghai: Shang-hai ku-chi, 1987). Trans. David Hawkes and John Minford, *The Story of the Stone*, five volumes (Harmondsworth: Penguin, 1973–86).

7. See Liu Hsiu-yeh, *Ku-tien hsiao-shuo hsi-ch'ü ts'ung-k'ao; (Beijing-Tsuo-chia, 1958)*. Chih-ts'ing Hsia's *The Classic Chinese Novel* (New York: Columbia University Press, 1968); and the introduction to Andrew

Plaks's *The Four Masterpieces of the Ming Novel: Ssu ta ch'i-shu* (Princeton: Princeton University Press, 1987).

8. Meyer Howard Abrams, *Natural Supernaturalism* (New York: Norton, 1973), 68.

9. Chu Hsi (1130–1200) is the master of the School of the Way, *Tao-hsüeh* in the Sung Dynasty. His comments on the Four Books (*The Analects, The Great Learning, The Doctrine of Means,* and *Mencius*) and the Five Classics (*The Book of History, The Book of Songs, The Book of Rites, the Book of Changes,* and *The Spring and Autumn Annals*) were officially recognized as the basis of the imperial examination. As we know, the examination was the most important, if not the unique, ladder of success in traditional Chinese society, and The Four Books and the Five Classics are the "bibles" of Confucianism.

10. Hans-Georg Gadamer, *Wahrheit und Methode* (Tübingen: Mohr, 1966), 266.

11. Ernst Cassirer, *The Philosophy of the Enlightenment,* trans. Fritz Koelin and James Pettergrove (Princeton: Princeton University Press, 1957), 135.

12. Taking into account that *Gil Blas* is the only French work incontestably accepted as a picaresque novel, I use the word "descendants" to indicate a large number of French novels—mainly written in the seventeenth and eighteenth centuries—which can be said to be related to the picaresque tradition. See Richard Bjornson, *The Picaresque Hero in European Fiction* (Madison: University of Wisconsin Press, 1977). Such works include for example, Charles Sorel's *La Vraye Histoire comique de Francion,* Atain René Lesage's *Gil Blas,* Pierre Carlet de Marivaux's *La Vie de Marianne* and *Le Paysan parvenu,* perhaps including Denis Diderot's *Jacques le fatalist,* and some novels in Honoré de Balzac's *La Comédie humaine.*

13. See Didier Souiller's description: "Jacob (the hero of *Le Paysan parvenu*) sincerely loves the person who is the most capable of satisfying his ambition at a given moment." Didier Souiller, *Le Roman picaresque* (Paris: PUF, 1980), 90. Just the opposite is true of Valmont, the hero of *Les Liaisons dangereuses.* Valmont claims that he gladly speaks ill of one of his numerous lovers—the only one with whom he made love in order to obtain a personal favor.

14. See Joan DeJean, *Literary Fortifications: Rousseau, Laclos, Sade* (Princeton: Princeton University Press, 1984), 207.

15. See Yao Ling-hsi's *P'ing-wai chih-yen* (T'ien-chin: T'ien-chin shu-chü, 1940), 74, as well as a considerable number of recent works on both novels.

16. Van Gulik also underscores the importance of Ming erotic art in his book and tries to explain the phenomenon by the historical context. Robert Hans Van Gulik, *Sexual Life in Ancient China* (Leiden: Brill, 1961), 116.

17. Christopher Lasch, *The Culture of Narcissism* (New York: Norton, 1976), 70.

18. Instead of choosing one of Sade's novels, I preferred Laclos's libertine novel, which represents a milder version of sadism.

19. See DeJean, *Literary Fortifications*, 329.

20. See *The Golden Lotus* (3:57:472).

21. Rougement's description of the adventure of love in China in one of his footnotes is somehow aberrant: "The Chinese have married young, unions being arranged by parents, and for them the problem of love does not arise." Then, he quotes Leo Ferroro to say that Western love "to a Chinese psychiatrist might well appear as symptomatic of insanity." Denis de Rougement, *Love in the Western World*, trans. Montgomery Belgion (Princeton: Princeton University Press, 1983), 71.

22. René Girard, *Mensonge romantique et vérité romanesque* (Paris: Grasset, 1961), 11.

23. According to Anthony Wilden, "need" invokes "instinct" or "drive" that can be satisfied, and "desire" implies an ineffable void that can never be filled. Anthony Wilden, *System and Structure: Essays in Communication* (New York: Barnes and Noble, 1972), 23.

24. Sun Shu-yü, *Chin P'ing Mei ti yi-shu* (Taipei: Shih pao wen hua, 1979), 99.

25. This couplet in the "Land of Illusion" reappears throughout the book as a kind of refrain: "Truth becomes fiction when the fiction's true; Real becomes not-real where the unreal's real." Hawkes's translation (1:1:55).

26. Rougement, *Love in the Western World*.

27. The fairy Disenchantment states: "To enjoy sensuality is lust, to understand passion is even more lustful." *The Dream of the Red Chamber* (1:5:146).

28. Hawkes's translation (1:5:145).

29. See the fairy Disenchantment's statement. Ibid. (1:5:147).

30. See Yü Ying-shih, *Hung-lou meng ti liang-ke shih-chieh* (Taipei: Lien-ching, 1978), 45.

31. T'ang Hsien-tsu, *Mou-tan t'ing* (Beijing: Jen-min, 1978). Trans. Cyril Birch. *The Peony Pavilion* (Bloomington: Indiana University Press, 1980).

32. Harold Bloom, "The Breaking of Form," Bloom et al. *Deconstructionism and Criticism* (New York: Seabury, 1979), 22.

Chapter 1

1. Choderlos de Laclos, *Les Liaisons dangereuses, Oeuvres complètes* (Paris: Gallimard, *"Pléïade,"* 1979). The English version: Choderlos de Laclos, *Dangerous Acquaintances*, trans. Richard Aldington (Norfolk: James Laughlin, 1952). This libertine novel was written in 1782 in epistolary form. The book is mainly about two libertines; the Marquise de Merteuil and the Vicomte de Valmont. They play with the feelings of other people; or "honest people" as the two libertines call them ironically. Then, they write to each other to praise their own victories over their victims.

2. Lan-ling hsiao hsiao sheng, *Chin P'ing Mei tz'u-hua*, 5 vols. (Tokyo: Dai-an, 1963).

3. See the beginning of the Confucian writing *Great learning: Ta-hsüeh.* Andrew Plaks makes this point in *The Four Masterworks of the Ming Novel: Ssu ta ch'i-shu* (Princeton: Princeton University Press, 1987), 503.

4. Jean DeJean, *The Literary Fortification: Rousseau, Laclos, Sade* (Princeton: Princeton University Press, 1984), 75.

5. 2 Corinthians 13.

6. See Meyer H. Abrams, *Natural Supernaturalism* (New York: Norton, 1973), 68.

7. See Laurent Versini's preface in Laclos's *Oeuvres complètes.*

8. André Malraux, *Le Triangle noir* (Paris: Gallimard, 1970), 48. Also see Suellen Diaconoff, *Eros and Power in "Les Liaisons dangereuses:" A Study in Evil* (Geneve: Droz, 1979), 8.

9. At the beginning of the book, Laclos pretended that he was merely a publisher who edited some anonymous letters, instead of being the author. In his alleged publisher's note, he further claimed—naturally with a touch of irony: "Indeed, several of the characters he describes have such abominable morals that it is impossible to suppose they could have lived in our own century—that century of philosophy in which enlightenment, spreading on all sides, has rendered (as everyone knows) all men so worthy and all women so modest and reserved." "Publisher's Note," vii.

10. Take as examples La Comtess in *les Legs* and Araminte in *les Fausses Confidences*. Pierre Marivaux, *Théâtre complet* (Paris: Garnier, 1968), 303–37 and 359–417.

11. See *Les Liaisons dangereuses, Oeuvres complètes*, 3.

12. Christopher Lasch, *The Culture of Narcissism* (New York-Norton, 1979), 69–70.

13. "The Présidente, (the only one belonging to the bourgeois class. Important observation)." Charles Baudelaire, *Oeuvres complètes* (Paris: Gallimard, 1954), 99.

14. Norbert Elias, *The Civilizing Process: The History of Manners*, trans. Edmond Jephcott (New York: Urizen, 1978).

15. Anne-Marie Jaton, *Le Corps de la liberté* (Vienna: Age d'Homme, 1983), 108.

16. Georges Poulet, *Etudes sur le temps humain: la Distance intérieure* (Paris: Plon, 1952), 70–80.

17. Roger Laufer, *Style Rococo, style des lumières* (Paris: José, 1963), 142.

18. Jean-Jacques Rousseau, *Julie, ou La Nouvelle Héloïse, Oeuvres complètes*, Vol. 2 (Paris: Gallimard, "Pléiade," 1959), (1:4:10).

19. Georges Poulet, *Distance intérieure*, 73.

20. Laufer, *Style Rococo*, (139–40).

21. *Oeuvres complètes*, 1:60:94, 2:81:164, 3:113:249.

22. "This was in Monsieur Chélan's house, at a dinner of priests. After the parish priest had presented him as a prodigy of instruction, it happened to him to praise Napoleon passionately. He tied his right arm to the shoulder, claiming to have broken it while moving the trunk of a pine tree. He remained in this embarrassing position for two months.

After this penitence, he forgave himself." Stendhal, *Le Rouge et le noir* (Paris: Flammarion, 1964), 39.

23. Jean-Paul Sartre, *L'Etre et le néant: Essai d'ontologie phénoménologique* (Paris: Gallimard, 1943), 306.

24. See Jean Rousset, *Forme et signification* (Paris: Corti, 1962), 98, and Jean-Luc Seylaz, *"Les Liaisons dangereuses" et la création romanesque chez Laclos* (Paris: Minard, 1958), 147.

Chapter 2

1. The French novel written by Choderlos de Laclos in 1782, which I have studied in my first chapter. Laclos, *Les Liaisons dangereuses, Oeuvres complètes* (Paris: Gallimard, "Pléiade," 1979).

2. Lan-ling hsiao hsiao sheng, *Chin P'ing Mei tz'u-hua (The Golden Lotus)*, 5 vols (Tokyo: Dai-an, 1963). This novel was written approximately between 1568 and 1602. However, the first extant edition dates from 1617. In this chapter, all translations are my own. I would also like to mention a French translation appearing recently in the Pléiade series: *Fleur en Fiole d'Or (Jin Ping Mei)*, trans. André Levy (Paris: Gallimard, "Pléiade," 1985).

3. *Liang* is a Chinese unit of measure equal to approximately 50 grams.

4. The servants, including his wives, usually call Hsi-men "father," which is a substitute for "master." In my English translation, I leave the word "father" as it is in Chinese.

5. *Ch'ien* is a Chinese unit of measure equal to approximately 5 grams. Twelve *ch'ien* equal one *liang*.

6. *Li* is a Chinese unit of measure equal to half a kilometer.

7. Wu Ch'eng-en, *Hsi-yu chi, The Journey to the West*, trans. Anthony Yü (Chicago: University of Chicago Press, 1976). This novel of one hundred chapters was written in the sixteenth century. The story is about the pilgrimage of Tripitaka, or *T'ang San-tsang*, who, protected by his three disciples, finally succeeds in bringing the Buddhist *sutras* from the Paradise of the West to China.

8. *Yin* and *yang* mean two essences that compose all the elements in the world. They are opposite, but at the same time transmutable.

They can also signify the two sexes in a concrete sense. See *The I Ching or Book of Change*, trans. Richard Wilhelm (Princeton: Princeton University Press, 1967).

9. See *The Golden Lotus*, (3:49:223). The same passage has been quoted in David Roy's article, "A Confucian Interpretation of the *Chin Ping Mei*," Academia Sinica Conference, Literature Section, 39–61.

10. Paul Martinson, "Pao, Order, and Redemption. Perspectives on Chinese Religion and Society Based on a Study of the *Chin Ping Mei*," Ph.D. dissertation (University of Chicago, 1973), 59–126.

11. See Michel Foucault, *Histoire de la sexualité: La Volonté de savoir*, vol. 1 (Paris: Gallimard, 1976), 121–22.

12. The use of this expression by Liu-erh is no doubt self-ironical, since a turtle in Chinese also means a husband who has an adulterous wife.

13. René Girard, *Mensonge romantique et vérité romanesque* (Paris: Grasset, 1961), 22.

14. See Georg Lukacs, *Die Theorie des Romans* (Neuwied: Luchterhand, 1962).

15. Charlotte Furth, "Blood, Body and Gender: Medical Images of the Female Condition in China," *Chinese Science* (1986) 7:43–46.

16. See Sun Shu-yü, *Chin P'ing Mei ti yi-shu* (Taipei: Shih-pao wenhua, 1978), 99.

17. *Hao* is the name that people in ancient China used in a more or less formal context.

18. Confucius, trans. James Legge, *Confucian Analects, The Great Learning, the Doctrine of the Mean, The Chinese Classic*, vol. 1 (Hong Kong: Hong Kong University Press, 1960), 263–64.

19. Hsiao P'ing, ed. *Feng fu chi ch'i-t'a* (Beijing: Chung-hua, 1959).

20. Jacques Derrida, *Dissemination*, trans. Barbara Johnson (Chicago: University of Chicago Press, 1981), 343.

21. Jacques Lacan, *Ecrits: a Selection*, trans. Alan Sheridan (New York: Norton, 1977), 285.

22. This is however commonplace in Chinese vernacular literature. In *Jou p'u-t'uan*, a seventeenth-century Chinese novel, the description is even cruder. Following the advice of a monk, the hero undergoes an

operation to amplify his organ with the assistance of that of a dog. See Li Yü (supposed author), *Jou p'u t'uan*, trans. Richard Martin, *The Prayer Mat of Flesh* (New York: Grove, 1963), chapter 8. And also in some *hua-pen* short stories, the attractiveness of a man is measurable by the dimension of his penis.

23. Lacan, *Ecrits: a Selection*, 288.

24. Derrida, *Dissemination*, 364.

25. As Charlotte Furth indicates in her article, "Blood, body and Gender," male "essence" or semen, at this period in China, was considered to be made of blood.

Chapter 3

1. Jean-Jacques Rousseau, *Julie, ou La Nouvelle Héloïse, Oeuvres complètes*, vol. 2 (Paris: Gallimard, "Pléiade," 1959). The English quotations are mostly from *Julie, or the New Eloise*, translated and abridged by Judith H. McDowell (University Park: Pennsylvania State University Press, 1968). In cases where I cannot find a passage, the translation is my own.

2. This eighteenth-century Chinese novel was written by Ts'ao Hsüeh-ch'in. The book is about an adolescent boy, Chia Pao-yü growing up together with his female cousins in a large family garden. Ts'ao Hsüeh-ch'in and Kao E, *Hung-lou meng san-chia p'ing-pen*, 4 vols (Shanghai: Shang-hai ku chi, 1987). English translation: trans. David Hawkes and John Minford, *The Story of the Stone*, 5 vols (Harmondsworth: Penguin, 1973–86)

3. Molière, *Oeuvres*, vol. 2 (Paris: Charpentier, 1889), 191.

4. Eugene Vance, "The Châtelain de Coucy: Enunciation and Story in Trouvère Lyric," *Marvelous Signals* (Lincoln: University of Nebraska Press, 1986), 51–85.

5. Tony Tanner is no doubt right in qualifying the scene of Julie being beaten by her father as the most physical, because the sexual relationship between the two lovers is mostly described in abstract terms. See Tony Tanner, "La Maison paternelle," in *Adultery in the Novel: Contract and Transgression* (Baltimore: Johns Hopkins University Press, 1979), 120–33. Before Tanner, other critics had also paid attention to the same problem. Jean Howard Hagstrum, for example, points out in his *Sex and Sensibility*, that the relationship between Julie and her father is "eroti-

cized" in this scene. See Jean Howard Hagstrum *Sex and Sensibility* (Chicago: University of Chicago Press, 1980), 229.

6. Jacques Derrida, *De la grammatologie* (Paris: Minuit, 1967), 203–34.

7. See Derrida: "Without the possibility of difference, the desire of presence as such would not find its breathing space. That means by the same token that this desire carries in itself the destiny of its nonsatisfaction. Difference produces what it forbids, makes possible the very thing that it makes impossible." Derrida, *Of Grammatology*, trans. Gayatri Chakravorty Spivak (Baltimore: Johns Hopkins, 1974), 143.

8. Jean-Jacques Rousseau, *Discours sur l'origine de l'inégalité parmi les hommes, Oeuvres complètes*, vol. 1 (Paris: Librairie Hachettè, 1884), 79.

9. Jean Baudrillard, *De la séduction* (Paris: Galilée, 1979), 105.

10. Jean Starobinski, *Jean Jacques Rousseau, La Transparence et l'obstable* (Paris: Gallimard, 1971), 413.

11. Rousseau, *Discours sur l'origine de l'inégalité parmi les hommes*, 102–03.

12. The translation is mine from the French edition. (4:6:422)

13. Victor Marguerite, *Jean-Jacques et L'amour* (Paris: Flammarion, 1926), 208–31.

14. My translation. See the French version. (6:8:693–94)

15. See Abrams, *Natural Supernaturalism* (New York: Norton, 1973), 68.

16. The translation is mine from the French version. (5:5:590)

17. See St. Augustine, *On the Trinity*, in *Basic Writings of St. Augustine*, vol. 2. ed. Whitney Oates (New York: Random House, 1948).

18. Lacan, *Ecrits: a Selection*, 2.

19. DeJean, *Literary Fortifications* (Princeton: Princeton University Press, 1984), 189.

20. Pierre Abelard, trans. Scott Moncrieff, *The Letters of Abelard and Héloïse* (New York: Knopf, 1942), 13.

21. My translation from the French version. (3:18:340)

22. My translation from the French version. (4:14:509)

23. My translation from the French version. (4:14:509)

24. Benveniste, *Problèmes de linguistique générale,* vol. 1 (Paris: Gallimard, 1966), 315.

25. Ste. Theresa or Teresa de Cepeda y Ahumada (1515–1582). Spanish, founder of covent St. Joseph and other female covents. Author of *The Way of Perfection, Thoughts on "The Song of Songs."*

26. Carl Schmitt, *Political Romanticism,* trans. Guy Oakes (Cambridge: The MIT Press, 1986), 17.

27. Ernest Bloch, "Processus et structure," *Entretiens sur les notions de Genèse et structure,* eds. Maurice de Gandillac, Lucien Goldmann, and Jean Piaget (Paris: Mouton, 1965), 228.

Chapter 4

1. Ts'ao Chan (1715/16?–1763/64?) is commonly kown by one of his courtesy names or *hao,* Ts'ao Hsüeh-ch'in, used in the first chapter of this book as that of an editor. His other *haos* are Ch'in-p'u, Meng-juan, and Ch'in-hsi Chü-shih. Despite the immense popularity of his work, the author's life remains obscure, even though a large number of articles and books are devoted to his life, especially in the Peoples Republic of China.

2. The textual analysis is based on Ts'ao Hsüeh-ch'in and Kao E, *Hung lou meng: (San-chia p'ing-pen)* 4 vol (Shanghai: Shang-hai Ku-chi, 1987). For the English version, I basically use David Hawkes' translation. *The Story of the Stone,* trans. David Hawkes and John Minford, 5 vols. (Harmondsworth: Penquin, 1973–1986).

3. Hsün K'uang, *Hsün-tzu chi shih,* ed. Li Ti-sheng (Taipei: T'ai-wan hsüeh-sheng, 1979), 506.

4. See chapter 2, endnote 21, s.

5. Chuang-tzu (or Chuang Chou), one of the most important writers of Taoist philosophy, lived approximately in the fourth century B.C. His book is called *Nan-hua ching* or *Chuang-tzu.* Trans. Angus Charles Graham, *The Seven Inner Chapters and Other Writings from the Book of Chuang-tzu* (London: Allen, 1981).

6. Hawkes translates *Ta-kuan yüan* as the Prospect Garden. This is somehow misleading, since *Ta-kuan* means a great view, including different sights in both heaven and on earth. A verse by the oldest sister of

the hero, Yüan-ch'un, who is an imperial concubine describes this. "Every sight in heaven and on earth is in the garden,/Which should be given the name of 'great view.' " Most of the hero's unmarried cousins and their maids live in the garden. Pao-yü is the only male inhabitant in this "paradise of girls."

7. Lucien Miller, *Mask of Fiction in "Dream of the Red Chamber": Myth, Mimesis and Persona* (Tuscon: University of Arizona Press, 1975), 57.

8. This beginning does not appear in the 120-chapter version. This is my own translation. According to Ch'en Yü-p'i, this part belongs to the general comments written by Chih-yen chai, mistakenly taken as the beginning of the original. See Ch'en Yü-p'i, *"Hung Lou meng shih tsen-yang k'ai-t'ou ti?"* (How does *The Dream of the Red Chamber* begin?) *Chung-hua wen shih lun ts'ung*, vol. 3 (Beijing: Chung-hua shu-chü, 1963), 333–38. However, in view of the intimate relationship between Chih-yen Chai and the author, this beginning can still be taken as another voice of the author which appears in the margins of the text.

9. See Hsün-tzu's "On the Rectification of Names," *Cheng-ming p'ien, Hsün-tzu chi shih*, Hsun-tzu, 503–35.

10. Chuang-tzu. Graham's translation, *The Seven Inner Chapters*, 75.

11. "The Red Dust" (*hung ch'en*) is the Buddhist term for the human world.

12. *Chuang-tzu*, Graham's translation, *The Seven Inner Chapters*, 61.

13. Ts'ao Hsüeh-ch'in, *Hung lou meng san-chia p'ing pen*, 3.

14. Ch'in K'e-ch'ing is the wife of Chia Jung, Hsi-feng's nephew.

15. Hsün-tzu, *"Cheng-ming p'ien," Hsün-tzu chi shih*. 505–35.

16. Yü Ying-shih, *Hung-lou meng ti liang-ke shih-chieh* (Taipei: Lien-ching, 1978), 50. For the overall structure of the garden, also see Andrew Plaks' chapter, "A Garden of Total Vision: the Allegory of the Ta-Kuan Yüan," *Archetype and Allegory in "The Dream of the Red Chamber"* (Princeton: Princeton University Press, 1976), 178–211.

17. See Yü ying-shih's *Hung Lou meng ti Liang-ke shih-chieh*, 53.

18. Hayden White, *Metahistory: The Historical Imagination in Nineteenth-century Europe* (Baltimore: Johns Hopkins University Press, 1973), 129.

19. Lan-ling hsiao hsiao sheng, *Chin P'ing Mei tz'u hua* (Tokyo Dai-an, 1963), 4:61:18.

20. Georges Bataille, *L'Erotisme* (Paris, Minuit, 1957), 119.

21. Hsü Hsiu-jung, ed. *Hung-lou meng chüan* (Taipei: Li-jen, 1981), 142.

22. Lu Hsün, *Lu Hsün ch'uan chi*, vol. 4 (Beijing: Jen-min wen hsüeh, 1961), 164.

23. Etymologically, (*yin*) is related to water, as in "inundation" (*yin-shui*), or "excessive rain" (*yin yü*). It also means excessive, evil, and misleading. In *Tsuo-chuan*, (*yin*) is defined as lust "*Yin* means greedy for sensuality," (*hao se wei yin*), *Tz'u-hai: yü-tz'u pu-fen*, vol. 1 (Shanghai: Tz'u-shu, 1980), 1017.

24. T'ang Hsien-tsu, *Mou Tan T'ing* (Beijing: Jen-min, 1978), 1.

25. Harold Bloom, "The Breaking of Form," Bloom et al, *Deconstructionism and Criticism* (New York: Seabury, 1979), 3–4.

26. Wang Shih-fu (1295–1307), *The Romance of the Western Chamber*, (Hsi-hsiang chi,) trans. S. I. Hsiung (New York: Columbia University Press, 1968).

27. Wong Kam-ming, "The Narrative Art of *Red Chamber Dream* (*Hung lou meng*)" Dissertation (Cornell, 1974), 177.

28. Sigmund Freud, trans. James Strachey, *Civilization and Its Discontents* (New York: Norton, 1961), 63.

29. To borrow the sarcastic word of Yü-ch'uan, a maid whose sister has killed herself after being accused by Pao-yü's mother of having seduced her boy. (2:43:361)

Bibliography

Abelard, Pierre. Trans. Scott Moncrieff. *The Letters of Abelard and Héloïse.* New York: Knopf, 1942.

Abrams, Meyer Howard. *Natural Supernaturalism.* New York: Norton, 1973.

Augustine, Saint, Bishop of Hippo. Ed. Whitney J. Oates. *On the Trinity. Basic Writings of St. Augustine.* Vol. 2. New York: Random House, 1948.

Bataille, Georges. *L'Erotisme.* Paris: Minuit, 1957.

————. Trans. Mary Dalwood. *Erotism: Death and Sensuality.* San Francisco: City Lights, 1986.

Baudelaire, Charles. *Oeuvres complètes.* Paris: Gallimard, "Pléiade," 1954.

Baudrillard, Jean. *De la séduction.* Paris: Galilée, 1979.

Benveniste. *Problèmes de linguistique générale.* Vol. 1. Paris: Gallimard, 1966.

Bjornson, Richard. *The Picaresque Hero in European Fiction.* Madison: University of Wisconsin Press, 1977.

Bloom, Harold. "The Breaking of Form." Bloom et al. *Deconstructionism and Criticism.* New York: Seabury, 1979.

Cassirer, Ernst. Trans. Fritz Koelin and James Pettergrove. *The Philosophy of the Enlightenment.* Princeton: Princeton University Press, 1957.

Certeau, Michel de. Trans. Brian Massumi. *Hetorologies: Discourse on the Other.* Minneapolis: University of Minnesota Press, 1986.

Ch'en Yü-p'i. *"Hung-Lou meng shih tsen-yang k'ai-t'ou ti?"* *Chung-hua wen-shih lun-ts'ung.* Vol. 3. Beijing: Chung-hua shu-chü, 1963, 333–38.

Chih-yen chai. *Chih-yen chai hung-lou meng chi-p'ing.* Shanghai: Wen-i lien-ho, 1954.

Chou Ju-ch'ang. *Hung-lou meng hsin-cheng.* Beijing: Jen-min, 1953.

Chuang-tzu. Trans. Angus Charles Graham. *The Seven Inner Chapters and Other writings from the Book of Chuang-tzu.* London: Allen, 1981.

Confucius. Trans. James Legge. *The Analects, The Great Learning, The Doctrine of the Mean. The Chinese Classics.* Vol. 1. Hong Kong: Hong Kong University Press, 1960.

DeJean, Joan. *Literary Fortifications, Rousseau, Laclos, Sade.* Princeton: Princeton University Press, 1984.

Deleuze, Gilles. *Logique du sens.* Paris: Minuit, 1969.

De Man, Paul. *Blindness and Insight: Essays in the Contemporary Criticism.* London: Methen, 1983.

Derrida, Jacques. *De la grammatologie.* Paris: Minuit, 1967.

————. Trans. Gayatri Chakravorty Spivak. *Of Grammatology.* Baltimore: Johns Hopkins University Press, 1974.

————. *Dissémination.* Paris: Seuil, 1972.

————. Trans. Barbara Johnson. *Dissemination.* Chicago: University of Chicago Press, 1981.

Diaconoff, Suellen. *Eros and Power in "Les Liaisons dangereuses": A Study in Evil.* Geneve: Droz, 1979.

Elias, Norbert. *Die Hôfishe Gesellschaft.* Newvied: Luchterhand, 1969.

————. Trans. Edmond Jephcott. *The Civilizing Process: The History of Manners.* New York: Urizen, 1978.

Felman, Shoshana. *La Scandale du corps parlant: Don Juan avec Austin ou la séduction en deux langues.* Paris: Seuil, 1980.

Foucault, Michel. *Histoire de la sexualité: La Volonté de savoir.* Vol. 1. Paris: Gallimard, 1976.

————. *Histoire de la sexualité: L'Usage des plaisirs.* Vol. 2. Paris: Gallimard, 1984.

————. *Histoire de la sexualité: Le Souci de soi.* Vol. 3. Paris: Gallimard, 1984.

Freud, Sigmund. Trans. James Strachey. *Civilization and Its Discontents.* New York: Norton, 1961.

Furth, Charlotte. "Blood, Body and Gender: Medical Images of the Female Condition in China." *Chinese Science* (1986): 7:43–46.

Gadamer, Hans-Georg. *Wahrheit und Methode.* Tübingen: Mohr, 1966.

Gandillac, Maurice de, Lucien Goldmann, et al. *Entretiens sur les notions de Genèse et structure.* Paris: Mouton, 1965.

Girard, René. *Mensonge romantique et vérité romanesque.* Paris: Grasset, 1961.

Gulik, Robert Hans van. *Sexual Life in Ancient China.* Leiden: Brill, 1961.

Hagstrum, Jean Howard. *Sex and Sensibility.* Chicago: Chicago University Press, 1980.

Hsia Chih-ts'ing. *The Classical Chinese Novel.* New York: Columbia University Press, 1968.

Hsiao P'ing, ed. *Feng-fu chi ch'i-t'a.* Beijing: Chung-hua, 1959.

Hsü Fu-kuan. *Chung-kuo yi-shu ching-shen.* Taipei: Chung-t'ai, 1966.

Hsü Hsiu-jung, ed. *Hung lou meng chüan.* Taipei: Li-jen, 1981.

Hsün K'uang. Ed. Li Ti-sheng. *Hsün-tzu chi shih.* Taipei: Tai-wan hsüeh-sheng, 1979.

Iser, Wolfgang. *The Act of Reading: A Theory of Aesthetic Response.* Baltimore: Johns Hopkins University Press, 1978.

Jaton, Anne-Marie. *Le Corps de la liberté.* Vienna: Age d'Homme, 1983.

Lacan, Jacques. *Les Quatre Concepts fondamentaux de psychanalyse.* Paris: Seuil, 1964.

————. *Ecrits I.* Paris: Seuil, 1966.

————. *Ecrits. II.* Paris: Seuil, 1971.

————. Trans. Alan Sheridan. *Ecrits: a Selection.* New York: Norton, 1977.

Laclos, Choderlos de. *Les Liaisons dangereuses. Oeuvres complètes.* Paris: Gallimard, "Pléïade," 1979.

————— . Trans. Richard Aldington. *The Dangerous Acquaintances*. Norfold: James Laughlin, 1952.

Lan-ling Hsiao-hsiao sheng. 5 vols. *Chin P'ing Mei tz'u-hua*. Tokyo: Dai-an, 1963.

————— . Trans. André Levy. *Fleur en Fiole d'Or (Jing Ping Mei)*. Paris: Gallimard, "Pléïde," 1985.

Lasch, Christopher. *The Culture of Narcissism*. New York: Norton, 1979.

Laufer, Roger.. *Style Rococo, style des lumières*. Paris: José, 1963.

Li Yü (supposed author). Trans. Richard Martin. *Jou p'u t'uan, The Prayer Mat of Flesh*. New York: Grove, 1963.

Liu Hsiu-yeh. *Ku-tien hsiao shuo hsi-ch'ü ts'ung k'ao*. Beijing: Tsuo-chia, 1958.

Lu Hsün. *Lu Hsün ch'uan chi*. Vol. 4. Beijing: Jen-min wen-hsüeh, 1961.

Luhmann, Niklas. Trans. Jeremy Gaines. *Love as Passion: The Codification of Intimacy*. Cambridge: Harvard University Press, 1986.

Lukas, Georg. *Die Theorie des Romans*. Neuwied: Luchterhand, 1962.

Malraux, André. *Le Triangle noir*. Paris: Gallimard, 1970.

Marguerite, Victor. *Jean-Jacques et l'amour*. Paris: Flammarion, 1926.

Marivaux, Pierre. *Théâtre complète*. Paris: Garnier, 1968.

Martinson, Paul. "Pao, Order, and Redemption: Perspectives on Chinese Religion and Society Based on a Study of the *CPM*." University of Chicago dissertation, 1973.

Mencius. Trans. James Legge. *The Works of Mencius. Chinese Classics*. Vol. 2. Hong Kong: Hong Kong University Press, 1960.

Miller, Lucien. *Mask of Fiction in "Dream of the Red Chamber": Myth, Mimesis and Persona*. Tuscon: University of Arizona press, 1975.

Molière. *Oeuvres*. Vol. 2. Paris: Charpentier, 1889.

Mote, Frederick. *Intellectual Foundations of China*. New York: Knopf, 1971.

Plaks, Andrew. *Archetype and Allegory in "The Dream of the Red Chamber"*. Princeton: Princeton University Press, 1976.

————— . *The Four Masterworks of the Ming Novel: Ssu ta ch'i-shu*. Princeton: Princeton University Press, 1987.

Poulet, Georges. *Etudes sur le temps humain: la Distance intérieure*. Paris: Plon, 1952.

Reiss, Timothy. *The discourse of Modernism*. Ithaca: Cornell University Press, 1982.

Rougement, Denis de. *L'Amour et l'Occident*. Paris: Plon, 1939.

————. Trans. Montgomery Belgion. *Love in the Western World*. Princeton: Princeton University Press, 1983.

Rousseau, Jean-Jacques. *Discours sur l'origine de l'inégalité parmi les homme. Oeuvres complètes*. Vol. 1. Paris: Librairie Hachette, 1884.

————. *Confessions. Oeuvres complètes*. Vol. 1. Paris: Gallimard, "Pléiade," 1959.

————. *Julie, ou La Nouvelle Héloïse. Oeuvres complètes*. Vol. 2. Paris: Gallimard, "Pléiade," 1959.

————. Trans. Judith H. McDowell. *Julie, or the New Eloise*. University Park: Pennsylvania State University Press, 1968.

Rousset, Jean. *Forme et signification*. Paris: Corti, 1962.

Roy, David. "A Confucian Interpretation of the *CPM*." *Academia Sinica Conference. Literature Section*. 39–61.

Sartre, Jean-Paul. *L'Etre et le néant: Essai d'ontologie phénoménologique*. Paris: Gallimard, 1943.

Schmitt, Carl. Trans. Guy Oakes. *Political Romanticism*. Cambridge: The MIT Press, 1986.

Seylaz, Jean-Luc. *"Les Liaisons dangereuses" et la création romanesque chez Laclos*. Paris: Minard, 1958.

Shih Nai-an. *Chung-yi shui-hu ch'uan chuan*. Shanghai: Ssu-lien, 1955.

————. Trans. Sidney Shapiro. *Outlaws of the Marsh*. Bloomington: Indiana University Press: 1981.

Souiller, Didier. *Le Roman picaresque*. Paris: PUF, 1980.

Starobinski, Jean. *Jean-Jacques Rousseau, La Transparence et l'obstable*. Paris: Gallimard, 1971.

Stendhal. *Le Rouge et le noir*. Paris: Flammarion, 1964.

Sun Shu-yü. *Chin p'ing mei ti yi-shu*. Taipei: Shih pao wen hua, 1979.

T'ang Hsien-tsu. *Mou-tan t'ing*. Beijing: Jen-min, 1978.

———. Trans. Cyril Birch. *The Peony Pavilion*. Bloomington: Indiana University Press, 1980.

Tanner, Tony. *Adultery in the Novel: Contract and Transgression*. Baltimore: Johns Hopkins University Press, 1979.

Ts'ao Hsüeh-ch'in (or Cao Xue-qin) and Kao E (or Gao E). *Hung lou meng: san-chia p'ing-pen*. 4 vols. Shanghai: Shang-hai ku-chi, 1987.

———. Trans. David Hawkes and John Minford. *The Story of the Stone*. 5 vols. Harmondsworth: Penguin, 1973–86.

Tu, Wei-ming. *Neo-Confucian Thought in Action, Wang Yang-ming's Youth (1472–1509)*. Berkeley: University of California Press, 1976.

Vance, Eugene. "The Châtelain de Coucy: Enunciation and Story in Trouvère Lyric." *Marvelous Signals*. Lincoln: University of Nebraska Press, 1986.

Versini, Laurent. *Laclos et la tradition*. Paris: Klinksieck, 1968.

Wang Shih-fu. Trans. S. I. Hsiung. *The Romance of the Western Chamber*. New York: Columbia University Press, 1968.

Wang Yang-ming (Wang Shou-jen). *Ch'uan Hsi lu*. Taipei: Shang-wu, 1967.

———. Trans. Wingtsit Chan. *Instructions for Practical Living and Other Neo-Confucian Writings by Wang Yang-ming*. New York: Columbia University Press, 1963.

Wei Tzu-yün. *Chin p'ing mei t'an-yüan*. Taipei: Shang-wu, 1979.

White, Hayden. *Metahistory: The Historical Imagination in Nineteenth-Century Europe*. Baltimore: Johns Hopkins University Press, 1973.

Wilden, Anthony. *System and Structure: Essays in Communication*. New York: Barnes and Noble, 1972.

Wilhelm, Richard, trans. *The I Ching or Book of Change*. Princeton: Princeton University Press, 1967.

Wong Kam-ming. "The Narrative Art of *Red Chamber Dream* (*Hung lou meng*)." Cornell dissertation, 1974.

Wu Ch'eng-en. Trans. Anthony Yü. *Hsi-yu chi, The Journey to the West*. Chicago: University of Chicago Press, 1976.

Wu Han. "*Chin p'ing mei ti chu-tsuo shih-tai chi-ch'i she-hui pei-ching*." *Tu shih cha-chi*. 1933, rpt. Peking: San-lien, 1961.

Wu Shih-ch'ang. *On the Red Chamber*. Oxford: Oxford University Press, 1961.

Yao Ling-hsi. *P'ing-wai chih-yen*. T'ien-chin: T'ien-chin shu-chü, 1940.

Yü Ying-shih. *Hung-lou meng ti liang-ke shih-chieh*. Tai-pei: Line-ching, 1978.

L

Lacan, Jacques, 1, 79, 106
Land of Illusion, 12, 141–42, 144, 163–64
Language, 87, 90, 92; ambiguity of, 131–32, 150–51; and differentiation, 130–31; and feeling, 91–92; inadequacy of, 171; of love, 14, 129–30, 132, 160; and recovery of the past, 93; and subversion, 154–55. *See also* Writing
Language, absurd, 131
Language, religious: as erotic, 11
Lasch, Christopher, 6, 22
Laufer, Roger, 27
Les Liaisons dangereuses, 2, 5, 6, 7, 15–44, 53, 62, 65, 66, 70, 85, 171
Libertinism, 17–18, 28, 37, 38–39, 104; and materiality, 7–8; as transgression, 45
Ling-ch'i. See Essence, sublime
Ling-hsing. See Essence, sublime
Love, 90, 92, 167; as absorption, 114–16; artificiality of, 47; idealization of, 9; linguistic ambiguity of, 82; linguistic reconstruction of, 82, 84; as obligation, 124; and power, 125; and reading, 86; as redemption, 114; rhetoric of, 81; and social status, 112–13; of self, 115–16; sublimation of, 8; as warfare, 85, 86. *See also* Desire; Passion
Love, preromantic, 104
Love, spiritual, 102
Lu Hsün, 159
Lukacs, Georg, 69
Lust, 162–66; linguistic ambiguity of, 12–13, 82

M

Madness: and passion, 158
Malraux, André, 16
Martinson, Paul, 60
Masochism, 40–41, 86, 108, 118
Memory, 98–100, 102, 121
Menstruation, 72
Miller, Lucien, 133
The Mirror for the Romantic, 135–36
The Mirror of Wind and Moon, 135–36
Misanthropy, 84–85
Misunderstanding, 161
Molière, 84, 89
Money, 53, 54, 55–59, 56; and morality, 59, 60
Morality, 53

N

Names, 75; emptiness of, 68, 69; irony of, 139; as linguistic signs, 130; and love, 139; and social authority, 147; and substance, 130, 131; undermined, 155. *See also* Naming
Naming, 74; in Confucianism, 130; and power, 47–48; and social order, 74–75. *See also* Names
Narcissism, 86, 98, 103, 110–12, 116, 121
Narcissus, 110
Nihilism, 127
Novel: erotic, 164–65; evolution of, 2; romantic, 164–65
Novel, Chinese: "chapter-divided novel," 2; formal conventions, 2
Novel, French: influence of Enlightenment on, 3, 4–5